Traveling Hopefully

Reflections for Pilgrims in the Fast Lane

Stan Mooneyham

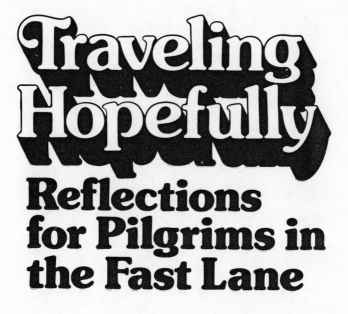

WORD BOOKS
PUBLISHER
WACO, TEXAS

A DIVISION OF
WORD, INCORPORATED

Library of Congress Cataloging in Publication Data

Mooneyham, W. Stanley, (Walter Stanley), 1926–
    Traveling hopefully.

    1 Meditations,   I. Title.
BV4832.2.M566   1984   248.4   83–23599
ISBN 0-8499-0345-9

Quotations marked LB, NIV, NEB, KJV, TEV and AB etc.
Printed in the United States of America

First Printing, February 1984
Second Printing, August 1984

to
Pilgrim

Contents

Foreword

This is not the book I wanted to write.

For more than a decade, I've wanted to say something about my pilgrimage as a human being and as a Christian. Understandably, I wanted to say something significant—which may be why I never got around to actually writing.

I started two or three times, but each time I had the distinct sense that I wasn't ready. Every time I started thinking about it, I found myself shooting at a moving target (myself) and I couldn't get a fix on me. So I kept waiting until I had arrived somewhere before trying to describe where I had been—and what had happened along the way.

But, distressingly, I seemed never to arrive.

·I remember a series of articles that *The Christian Century* carried from time to time. They were written by prominent churchmen and theologians under the title, "How My Mind Has Changed." It was no surprise that the editors never asked me for a contribution, but that didn't keep me from wanting to make my own statement. The trouble was that the longer I waited, the more I was sure the only authentic piece I could write was, "How My Mind Keeps Changing." But such a book

would have been obsolete before it was published. So I
haven't yet written the book I want to write.

In the meantime, however, I have discovered something
about my pilgrimage. The first thing is that I will arrive
somewhere only if I stop moving (read "growing"). As Robert
Raines says, "The Bible is about journeys and pilgrims," not
arrivals. The second is that my pilgrimage is not a smooth
ride down a freeway in a Cadillac with automatic transmis-
sion. It is more like my boyhood rides in a sputtering Model T
Ford over bumpy rural Mississippi roads.

Progress is measured more by fits and spurts than by the
quiet click of an odometer. But never mind. I came to identify
with Robert Louis Stevenson's belief, "To travel hopefully is
a better thing than to arrive."

So I struggled on, in hope. And instead of writing the book I
wanted to write, I have written the only book I could write. It
is a series of essays or thought vignettes written over a period
of three years. They first appeared in *World Vision* magazine
as a signed column titled "Words on the Way." In compiling
them for this volume, however, I have felt the need to re-
phrase and edit some of the earlier ones. In the interim since
they were written, I have grown in understanding and developed new perceptions.

In retrospect, I realize these essays do measure much of my
pilgrimage. As my vistas have enlarged through God's gift of
improved spiritual sight, I see things I never saw before—and
my perspective on other things has changed. As a result, I am
able to share with you on these pages—at some risk—my
search for authenticity as regards myself, my relationships,
my work, and my eternal hope.

Generally speaking, that is not safe. To question conven-
tional evangelical wisdom, I have discovered, is to risk rejection by your peers. To expose your struggles, especially if you
are a "leader," is to risk misunderstanding by virtually everyone. Leaders are supposed to have it all together. Almost all
the authority figures on the American evangelical scene today

project the image of having no uncertainties about anything.

Maybe they don't—but I do. For me to portray any other image would be phony, and I can't do that while I'm struggling to be real.

In my mid-50s, I see more of life's ambiguities than I did when I was a university sophomore. Then, the things for which I did not have authoritative answers were scarcely worth bothering with! But the experience of years has changed that. Now, I have more questions and fewer answers.

As peripheral things dropped away, this allowed me to focus more clearly on the central core of my beliefs. The result is that I am absolutely certain of fewer things, but of the things that remain, I am more certain than ever before. And those things have to do with life's basic issues—who Jesus is, who I am, the value of other people, and God's sovereignty in my life.

About those things, I shall not be moved.

As for all the rest, I want to keep testing everything. When television commentator Eric Severeid retired in 1977, prominent on a list of things he said he had learned in a half-century as a journalist was this: "To retain the courage of one's doubts, as well as one's convictions, in this world of dangerously passionate certainties."

Yes.

I don't believe heaven is shook up over my lingering questions. I think God can cope. I hope my brothers and sisters can.

Now I affirm people more and my convictions less.

I owe an extraordinary debt of gratitude to Dr. Kenneth Wilson, a colleague who has traveled with me—geographically and emotionally—through many of my deep struggles. He empathized with me and comforted me when the waters got neck high. I have found in Ken, a former editor of *Christian Herald*, a fellow pilgrim. His involvement in this volume has been in every step of the process—from the stimulation of ideas to the choice of words for their articulation.

So many others deserve mention that it would be impossible to name them all even if I could remember them. Some of them are anonymous fellow pilgrims I have met along the way. Others are part of an intimate friendship group, which has compassionately helped steady and shape my life. These special people have done this not by being strong, but by daring to let me see their weaknesses. A select few have been unusually caring on a one-to-one basis. For the most part, these are old friends who don't feel threatened when I share a disturbing idea. Some are newer friends, but with them, too, the trust level is very high.

I affirm Sarah Jewett's view: "Old friends is always best, 'less you can catch a new one that's fit to make an old one out of."

Maybe someday I'll write the book I want to write. Then again, I may never. It doesn't really matter. I'm sure the next time will be the same as this time. I will write what I am able to write at that semi-colon point in my pilgrimage.

But whichever, I hope you will sense about this volume what John Chancellor said about Eric Severeid: "He never told people what he thought, but what he learned."

For me, the best learning takes place on the road, not at the inn. Maybe that is why Jesus affirmed himself not as the destination, but the way.

So travel on, pilgrim. May we meet at various waystops to share the learnings of the road, be it a shady path or the fast lane.

In search of one's own self

The man talking to the reporter from the *Los Angeles Times* was identified as "a friend and board member" of the head of an evangelistic empire, whom he was describing: "When he's not on stage, he's intelligent, reasonable, logical, and perceptive. But he's on stage too much."

He is, in other words, a role player.

He is not alone. I can identify with him as, I suspect, can many other Christian public personalities. The difference between the role and the real probably causes many of us some sleepless nights.

Since being ordained into the Christian ministry at twenty-one, I have been more or less a "public person" with responsibilities which made it difficult ever to develop a private self. Men of the cloth are particularly susceptible, I think, although not exclusively vulnerable.

I had a strange sense of *deja vu* as I read the *Time* cover story about actor Peter Sellers (March 3, 1980). Appearing on The Muppet Show, he was told by Kermit the Frog that it was all right to "just relax and be yourself." To which Sellers replied, "I could never be myself. You see, there is no me. I do not exist."

Acknowledging that it was a good joke, *Time* saw a deeper significance: "The real Peter Sellers, at 54, is virtually a cipher." The magazine quoted a longtime friend as saying, "Peter is the accumulation of all the roles he's played and all the people he's met. He's directing traffic inside all that."

Sellers died less than six months later. I don't know if he ever found himself. Nor do I know if, indeed, he ever searched for himself, although I suspect he may have. There is something inside us that yearns for discovery—even when it has been submerged for years. In part, at least, that is probably what the "mid-life crisis" is all about—the need to know ourselves before we go to our graves.

Thomas Merton believed ". . . the problem of sanctity and salvation is in fact the problem of finding out who I am and of discovering my true self." Equally profound is this statement by an anonymous young man: "I could know myself better if there weren't so many of me."

Some of these multiple personalities inside us exist as simultaneous roles. Others have been covered over and forgotten as roles changed. The recovering of authenticity means resolving the conflicting personalities as well as taking off the layers of wallpaper. Removing old wallpaper is, as anyone who has done it knows, a disagreeable task that yields only to persistence. I had just about forgotten some of those old patterns, applied so neatly through some thirty-five years of public ministry.

On reflection, I can see now that sometimes the role, the task to be done, does contribute a mystique, an enabling of its own. For example, upon some of its occupants, the White House has imparted a quality of leadership they did not have when they moved in. Why didn't it work for all? Perhaps because some of the men became amplified through honest versions of themselves, while others were trying to look and act as they thought a president should look and act.

But whether president or pauper, how do you go about recapturing genuineness? First, it takes a new kind of trust in

God's presence and power. God leaves us free to be whatever we like. He does not clone human beings, but he gives each of us a unique, authentic self—and then encourages us to discover it, nurture it and expose it to others. However, we often find a familiar mask to be more secure than an unknown reality, especially if others approve the mask. Would they like *me* equally as much, we wonder? Probably. But it takes stepping over the frightening threshold of vulnerability to discover that the other side offers not hidden terrors, but the beginning of security.

Second, no person, I think, can come to truly know himself except through the process of disclosing himself to others. But that self-disclosure—removing the masks—can occur only in an atmosphere of love and trust. While it seems scary at first, it is more frightening to consider the consequences of continued pretense. Thomas Merton, the monk who excelled in the inner search, warns "If we have chosen the way of falsity, we must not be surprised that truth eludes us when we finally come to need it."

But when genuineness is adopted as a way of life, it means no longer having to pretend, and that means freedom to grow and fully serve. And that means unspeakable joy and serenity.

When you know who you are, you don't have to impress anyone. When Jesus was taken before the high priest, who asked, "What do you have to say for yourself?" (Mark 14:60 LB), Jesus was silent.

Wrong question.

When the high priest then asked him if he was the Son of God, Jesus said, "I am."

Right question.

Before Pilate, who asked, "Are you the King of the Jews?" Jesus replied, "Yes, it is as you say."

Right question.

In the Luke account, Herod "asked Jesus question after question, but there was no reply."

Wrong questions.

When you have discovered your identity, you need to say little else. Toyohiko Kagawa, the Japanese Christian who spent his life working with and for the poor, was speaking at Princeton. When he finished his talk, one student said to another, "He didn't say much, did he?"

A woman sitting nearby leaned over and murmured, "When you're hanging on a cross, you don't have to say anything."

Pilgrim's process

As nearly as I can tell, most Christians as well as secular people today are goal-oriented. It fits the American style. The less popular option is to be process-oriented, which I personally think is the better way to go. Just getting there is not all that counts. How you get there and what happens to you and to others along the way are at least equally important.

A couple of decades ago the Cunard Steamship Company advertised its cruises with the words "Getting there is half the fun." Maybe so. But I can tell you that sometimes getting there is no fun at all. Especially if you are imprisoned in the middle seat of a Boeing 747 for fourteen hours between San Francisco and Hong Kong.

Even on five-hour New York/Los Angeles flights, a valiant effort is made to narcotize passengers with food, drink, and motion pictures. I could never quite understand the logic of shutting the window curtains on the reality of the Grand Canyon outside so that Hollywood's latest make-believe would show up better on the screen inside.

That's not too surprising, though, because this is the way we often live our Christian lives. We get so absorbed with where we think we're going that we shut out sights and experiences, both glorious and painful, along the way.

The priest and Levite on the road from Jerusalem to Jericho were goal-oriented. On their minds were things other than a mugging victim. Perhaps important things. Maybe they were on their way to conduct all-Jericho evangelistic meetings or to lead a seminar on the family or to kick off a hunger campaign. The Samaritan of the parable was process-oriented. He, too, was on his way to Jericho, but for him getting there was not only less than half the fun but probably three-quarters of the pain. He saw not only the road, but the ditches alongside. He didn't pretend that he had not seen what he saw. He didn't try to convince himself that his goal down the road was more important than a deed of mercy to be transacted then and there.

In stopping and stooping he was not taking time out from his life; he was *living* his life.

Goals are points in time. Process is time itself. If winning were all there is to a baseball game, the game would need to last only one inning. Golf would take only one hole, a 100-yard dash, no more than fifteen feet. Obviously, in sports, a large part of the game is the playing, the savoring, the enduring, the lasting. Is it not as true in our Christian walk?

In one of his books, William Barclay tells the story of a group of people in the Scottish Highlands who were talking about heroism. Everyone, they said, sooner or later must practice some kind of heroism. A brash young man in the group turned to an old woman who looked ordinary and serene; he did not know that life for her had been a series of tragedies. "And what kind of heroism do you practice?" he asked lightly. "I?" she replied. "I practice the heroism of going on."

Bravo! Going on—lasting—*is* heroic. We demonstrate so little staying power. Most often we want to leapfrog, bypass, shortcut the process, when the process is what life is mainly about.

John Bunyan did not call his book *Pilgrim's Destination* but *Pilgrim's Progress*. He could as well have called it *Pilgrim's Process*. In the book, the central character named Christian was shaped by the road he traveled. He became ultimately what he was becoming all along. Jesus told Peter and Andrew, "Follow me and I will make you to become . . ." (Mark 1:17). It was not a promised overnight transformation. Every step along dusty Galilean roads, every encounter with need, every response to happenings, would be a bit of becoming.

Even in our attempts to shortcut and anesthetize, we are becoming. When we shut our eyes, stop our ears, try to shield ourselves from feeling our own pain or that of others, we are becoming. By his reaction to interruption, the Levite—as well as the Samaritan—was in the process of becoming a little more of something he had not as fully been.

Don't we, when we are goal-oriented, resent distractions and intrusions? The goal-directed disciples tried to "protect" Jesus from some children who were drawn to him. Jesus told the disciples the kingdom of heaven was not only around a distant turn in the road; a little sample was right in front of them. The disciples didn't know it. They thought to serve the Lord by irritably defending worthwhile goals, completely missing the need to demonstrate love and sensitivity in the process.

In our evangelical world, there is no lack of big projects. There is only a lack of big people who can work for God without trampling others along the way. The assumption too often is that if the goal is noble, the means need not be.

Goals are important. Of course they are. But the process is not less so. It would be sad indeed if the shining goal were spectacularly achieved but the way was littered with human debris put there by distorted zeal that had no room for the Christ the goal was meant to serve. But is it possible for a road littered with human wreckage ever to lead to a Christ-serving goal?

Although some ends are never reached, means are *always*

reached. Which causes me to wonder whether the process itself shouldn't *be* the goal. These are things I plan to think more about. Could we think about them together?

Coke is not the only real thing

I promised to do some more thinking about the process of living, remembering that believers were and are followers of the Way, not mere heedless seekers of the destination. As a result, I'm finding out a little more about living creatively and redemptively in the now.

When it comes to faith, I've observed, it is the present tense that is usually shortchanged. We do well on events that happened decently long ago. Why is it, I wonder, that a Golden Age of anything is always somewhere in the past? Why do we never recognize a Golden Age when we're in the midst of one? Many of us—churches, too—are living in the Land of Was, trying to recapture the glow of victories past, forever telling how it used to be.

Faith's futurism has also received more than its share of attention. We sing about a balm in some ethereal Gilead, scarcely conscious of divine ointment available for today's wounds. We lift paeans of praise to the Sweet By and By, but where is the soaring evangelical hymnody about the Nasty Here and Now—songs that make us feel it is an incomparable privilege to be alive, come what may?

This side of the Third World we have almost convinced

21

ourselves that, for Christians, the going isn't supposed to be rough; we're not supposed to become depressed, have marital problems, generation gaps, business failures, sorrows. Tragedy is something that happens to unbelievers, and if it does overtake the faithful, it is presumed to be embarrassing evidence of a flawed faith. So we engage in the Big Coverup, cloaking our humanity, our hurts, or failures—not under a mantle of love which we should do with the faults of others, but behind a curtain of self-protective deceit—because we cannot face the exposure of being honest and real.

Thus Christianity could be said to have its own Watergate—for whether the life is public or private, transparency is terrifying.

Much of what passes as Bible-believing, Spirit-filled evangelical piety is, I am convinced, little more than Christian role-playing. We act the way we think we are expected to act. We admit to nothing that tarnishes our self-projected image. We hide in past and future.

And inside, afraid to be real, we are crumbling.

Reality is not an abstraction. It is achievable only in specifics. It is what I am and you are at this moment, in this place, masks off. It is not something to escape from but to escape to. As frightening as the prospect of transparent honesty may appear, reality is not necessarily hostile. It can be friendly. At least, that is my experience. It is where healing must be found, where health must be lived out. It precludes refuge in the drug and alcohol scene or its religious equivalent.

Reality brings release and freedom as nothing else can, but it cannot be experienced apart from Jesus who gives us courage to take the first timorous step into our threatening Jordan Rivers, without which the waters of pretense and hypocrisy will not and cannot roll back.

The Velveteen Rabbit by Margery Williams (Doubleday), written for children but to my mind even more meaningful for role-playing adults, says it in gentle allegory:

"The Skin Horse had lived longer in the nursery than any of

the others. He was so old that his brown coat was bald in patches and showed the seams underneath, and most of the hairs in his tail had been pulled out. He was wise, for he had seen a long succession of mechanical toys arrive to boast and swagger, and by and by break their mainsprings and pass away, and he knew that they were only toys and would never turn into anything else.

" 'What is REAL?' asked the Rabbit one day, when they were lying side by side near the nursery fender, before Nana came to tidy the room. 'Does it mean having things that buzz inside you?'

" 'Real isn't how you are made,' said the Skin Horse. 'It's a thing that happens to you. When a child loves you for a long, long time, not just to play with, but REALLY loves you, then you become Real.'

" 'Does it hurt?' asked the Rabbit.

" 'Sometimes,' said the Skin Horse. 'When you are Real, you don't mind being hurt.'

" 'Does it happen all at once, like being wound up,' he asked, 'or bit by bit?'

" 'It doesn't happen all at once,' said the Skin Horse. 'You become. It takes a long time. That's why it doesn't often happen to people who break easily, or have sharp edges or who have to be carefully kept. Generally, by the time you are Real, most of your hair has been loved off and you get loose in the joints and very shabby. But these things don't matter at all, because once you are Real you can't be ugly, except to people who don't understand. Once you are Real you can't become unreal again. It lasts for always.' "

On my pilgrimage toward trying to become real, I have found much help in the writings of Henri J. M. Nouwen. In *The Wounded Healer*, this Catholic priest points out: "The Christian leader is not one who reveals God to his people— who gives something he has to those who have nothing—but one who helps those who are searching to discover reality as the source of their existence."

It is possible, I now believe, for a person to be the real thing. But don't expect to see mass conversions. It is still, as I perceive it, only for individual souls who find courage to make a start in spite of timidity and fear.

Most will prefer the anonymity and safety to be found behind a mask. Many will still choose the comfort of nostalgia. It is a nice place to visit, but I wouldn't want to live there. Others will continue to shortcut or leapfrog the painful present to find comfort in future hope. That is good to have, but we don't live there, either. Not yet.

For the rest of us, there is only today. The process of living this day is taking us somewhere. There *is* a destination. On this earth, I believe the destination is to become real. If we cannot reach that point here, and go on from there without pretense, how can God trust us with his heaven?

The tyranny of things

Every now and again I discover some pretty good theology coming out of modern songwriters. For one thing, their words are more comprehensible to me than what comes out of most theologians. My fault, I'm sure, not theirs, but still true. Now I don't know anything about Kris Kristofferson's faith, but you'd be hard pressed to find a more succinct statement of truth than this line in his song, *Me and Bobbie McGee:* "Freedom's just another word for nothin' left to lose."

I can just hear Jesus affirming that: "A man's life does not consist in the abundance of his possessions" (Luke 12:15 NIV).

I don't believe Jesus is taking a hard-line view of abundance. What he is saying is that the acquisition of things, contrary to general belief then and now, is not where life's true values reside. At issue is not the abundance or scarcity of things (Paul allowed that he was able to co-exist peacefully with either, see Phil. 4:12), but rather the importance one attached to things, many or few.

I suspect that for most of us, poor as well as rich, Christian as well as not, things are what our lives are mostly about. To the extent that this is so, we do not possess things but are possessed by them. We go through life harnessed to their

25

weight like Bryant's "quarry-slave at night" goes "scourged to his dungeon."

No freedom to skip and dance.

Reared in poverty, I've all my adult life had an emotional need for economic security. Looking back from this vantage point, I am appalled that I took so little time out to smell flowers or marvel at meadowlarks. For me, the butterflies were all queasily in my stomach, none gloriously on the wing. I, too, have bent under the burden, ever conscious of what little I had, unaware that it had me; worrying lest I lose even the little. Which is why I know Jesus was talking about an attitude, not an amount.

The crazy thing is that all the time I knew the text by heart. I used to quote it for others in sermons.

Lately, but perhaps not too late, I am learning that freedom from the tyranny of things means letting go, relinquishing the grasping, focusing attention on something other than getting and keeping.

A recent television program showed a method for trapping monkeys. The natives made a hole in a log and put bait inside. The monkey reached his hand in to get the bait, but when his fingers closed on it, he couldn't get his fist back through the hole. Determined to hang on to what he had, he was still hanging on when captured. All he needed to do to be free was let go. But to let go was to him incomprehensible—his priorities would not permit it.

So he is destroyed by what he supposes he possesses. Silly monkey. Silly people.

And it can happen with so little.

In his story of Russian prison camp experiences, Solzhenitsyn tells of inmates who suffer incredible hardships and have nothing but the barest of essentials, yet learn to be at peace. Then a rare gift parcel arrives with a few simple things. Immediately, the recipient becomes protective and withdrawn, jealously guarding each small item—an ugly mood, Solzhenitsyn says, worse than prison itself.

Try to recall how quickly the things we "possess" become meaningless when something really important comes along. When a serious illness strikes, it is immediately clear that life does not consist of things. When sirens and flashing lights signal an accident on the road, I think how suddenly life has changed for those involved. All plans and carefully set priorities are suddenly rearranged.

A friend told me the story of a traveler in a far country who was making a long journey by train. He put his valise on the overhead rack and having been warned to guard his bag at all times against thieves, he checked the rack frequently with his eyes.

Darkness fell, lights were turned on, the train clattered through the night. The traveler did not dare sleep for he had to watch his valise. By morning, he was bleary-eyed, but he had kept awake; his valise was secure. Keeping his eyes open became torture and despite his valiant efforts, they closed for a few moments. With a start, he awoke and looked up. The valise was gone. "Thank God," he sighed, "now I can go to sleep!"

The things which own us don't have to be just cars, houses and lands. Ideas, convictions and prejudices can possess our minds and attitudes. These are the worst kind of tyrants, I've discovered. They make us judgmental, quarrelsome, schismatic. They drive us to all kinds of spiritual excesses under the disguise of "truth." Often they are simply human biases, yet they demand uncritical loyalty even at the sacrifice of relationships.

When that happens, we no longer hold our convictions; they hold us. And they—at least, mine—tenaciously resist being tested against other, possibly higher, priorities. Though we may possess such ideas in abundance, they do not necessarily contribute to abundant living. Instead, our ideas restrict us, imprison us and subtract from our liberty as sons and daughters of God.

Giving another person space in which to grow—and make

mistakes while growing—requires greater trust than the more possessive of us are willing to give. Our unbending bias simply will not allow it. Yet there can be no spiritual reality for us or them without the risk.

Jesus was right. Life is more than meat and drink, houses and land, convictions and prejudices. It is also peace and contentment, love and trust, skipping and dancing. O yes. And meadowlarks.

God's will—good, better, best?

I recall hearing a famous preacher say, "To find the will of God is the greatest discovery; to do the will of God is the magnificent achievement."

That it was good theology I had no doubt. But no one could tell me for sure how to know the will of God and how to be sure I was doing God's will and not my own. Pointers, I got. And hints and suggestions.

However, it was communicated to me subtly, and sometimes not so subtly, that God had two wills for me. One was his *perfect* will, which I was urged to seek, find and do. But (and this was said almost in a whisper), if I aimed for the top and fell short, God would reluctantly grant me his *permissive* will. The implication was that beneath his perfect best for me are ranked his less desirable second best, third best, and so on.

I had no reason to question that concept at the time, but I do now for I see what it does. It shifts sovereignty from Creator to created. If that view is right, I can, by my disobedience, obstinance or ignorance, force God to fall back to a second or third line of action and to maneuver within whatever leeway I have left him. Furthermore, because "the will of God" in a given circumstance often cannot be precisely defined (we have inherited many of our problems and *any* solution will be less than perfect by our measure), many fear they may miss the will of God simply because they don't know a formula for finding it, thereby cheating themselves and handicapping God.

I don't think "best" and "next best" describe the way God works. I have found nothing in the Bible nor in my experience that validates this multi-will concept. It pushes both God's sovereignty and God's grace out of shape.

If he is sovereign, God is not dependent upon my ability to make right choices. A former colleague of mine used to say, "A Christian is the only person I know who can choose any one of four different directions and have it be right!" In my heart, I know he's right. It isn't that a "wrong" choice may accidentally turn out to be "right." It's that the grace of God redeems "wrong" choices.

Indeed, in the light of Romans 8:28, one must ask if there is such a thing as an unredeemable choice for one who loves God and is called according to his purpose. *All* things work together for good—wise decisions and unwise ones. Who, in fact, can be certain at the time which are which? And who at the time of decision-making can discern, except through faith, the good that is working together? Good, as we tend to recognize it, means plenty rather than want, comfort rather than discomfort, harmony rather than tension. But God seems to place more value on ultimate results than on short-term benefits.

Take the conflict between Paul and Barnabas over the young disciple, John Mark (Acts 15:36-41 NEB). Mark had disappointed Paul by turning back and failing to complete their first missionary journey, so Paul refused to take him again. "The dispute was so sharp that they parted company. Barnabas took Mark . . . Paul chose Silas."

Surely both these men were seeking God's will. I cannot believe that God caused the disagreement in order to separate them into two teams, thus making them twice as effective, and, not incidentally, bringing Timothy into the picture with Paul (16:3). I believe God redeemed the choices of two men who loved him. He used even their humanness, their temperaments—yes, their tempers. We will never know what would have happened had they not quarreled, but I am sure God was not placed at the mercy of their disagreement, and neither were they.

The Scriptures confirm that sometimes God does give direct guidance by the Holy Spirit. But if not, he does not allow "wrong" choices to go unredeemed. It can't be otherwise. If not, who would be willing to choose when faced by two paths at a fork in the road? We would be paralyzed with fear of making the wrong choice. Or having finally made a choice, we would live always with the agonizing possibility that the other path might have been better.

So, in grace, God redeems the choices of his children. That is what grace is—undeserved favor. God does not coerce me, manipulate me or violate my will. He does not play from a stacked deck. He respects the powers which he created within me. As one who loves him and is called according to his purpose, I am free to choose and God elects my choice to be right.

All of which says to me, "Love God, relax, and get on with the business of living!" The principle that God is sovereign over not only my life but my choices liberates me to live with assurance instead of apprehension that I may blow it.

Since I am free, I may indeed blow it. If I violate the principles of life which God has woven into the very fabric of the universe, I cannot escape the consequences. Choices do have consequences. David paid dearly for his sin even though God regarded him as "a man after his own heart" (1 Sam. 13:14). But God remained sovereign in the circumstances. Though God did not "elect" David to sin, the sovereign result was that Israel got Solomon, the wisest king in the nation's history.

When the potter remade the marred clay into "another vessel, as it seemed good . . . " (Jer. 18:4), he was not making something that was second best. The final product, according to the story, was still what the potter wanted to make.

God says we can expect him to do at least as much.

For me, it is more than enough.

Pastures—green and otherwise

Lying down in the green pastures of Psalm 23 has long been a favorite fantasy of mine. Especially when the nitty gritty of life wearies me.

I don't have much firsthand knowledge of the "valley of the shadow of death." Sometimes things seem to get that bad, but even then I remember that David talks about walking *through* the valley. That means sooner or later coming out on the other side, back into the sunlight. But on honest reflection, my problems are more your ordinary, garden variety than they are the "valley of the shadow" kind.

And I'm not much into the sweet revenge aspect of sitting down to a feast in the presence of my enemies, either. Also, it occurred to me that doing so seems a likely way to make enemies, even if you didn't have any to start with.

But I have to confess that the thought of those green pastures gets to me when the pressure cooker of life starts to heat up. That's when I want that meadow with cool breezes and fleecy clouds, a kind of spiritual Shangri-la where the troubles and trivia of the real world can't intrude.

Some people create such a place through the artificial means of alcohol or drugs. But since I choose not to anesthe-

tize myself that way, when I've been battered and wounded in
life's fray, I echo David's plaintive wish, "Oh, that I had the
wings of a dove to fly away and be at rest: I should escape far
away and find a refuge in the wilderness" (Ps. 55:6–8 NEB).

You, too?

My daughter, Robin, calls that "future tripping"—doing
anything to avoid living in the unpleasant present. Usually,
the experience takes the form of believing that the untroubled
meadow lies just beyond the present set of problems.

That's when I end up resenting the next intrusion of life's
reality. It is a feeling, I think, common to us all. The disciples
felt it. Matthew tells about the time that they had just come
back from a spiritual retreat with Jesus. Still feeling the eu-
phoria of those unhurried days, they resented the multitudes
of sick and hungry people. "Send the crowds away" (Matt.
14:15 LB), they said to Jesus irritably.

A short time later, a woman upset them with her insistent
pleading on behalf of a sick daughter. " 'Tell her to get going,'
they said, 'for she is bothering us with all her begging'"
(Matt. 15:23 LB).

Messy realities got in the way of their ideas about how life
should be spent. So did little children. Matthew says ". . . the
disciples scolded those who brought them. 'Don't bother
him,' they said" (19:13 LB), but I wonder who was really bothered. To Jesus, little children were not digressions from his
agenda. They *were* the agenda. Of the crowds, he said, "I don't
want to send them away . . ." (Matt. 15:32 LB).

Sick and hungry people and distraught mothers and wet
diapers were not intrusions into life. They were what real life
was about.

Or, to put it another way: "Life is what happens to you
while you are making other plans."

My guess is that the Good Samaritan wasn't overjoyed at
the sight of a wounded man on the roadside. He likely had a
time schedule to meet and important appointments in
Jericho. The two religious types who had preceded him and

"passed by on the other side" might spiritualize their neglect of the beaten traveler, but for the Samaritan it was all part of his real life. Facing a choice, he chose the interruption.

Looking back at my life, the events I remember best and which turned out to be the most glorious blessings, are those which at the time seemed to be traumatic interruptions. Our youngest son was an unplanned interruption. Conversion, for many of us, was an interruption of carefully laid intentions. Whatever it was, after it happened, the original agenda seemed less important.

Reflect for a moment on Henry Thoreau's statement in *Walden's Pond*: "We now no longer camp as for a night, but have settled down on earth and forgotten heaven." I've wanted to turn many of my green pastures into permanent estates, but a meadow with buildings is no longer a meadow.

And a pilgrim who lives on an estate is no longer a pilgrim. Tent-dwellers can't program green pastures. You can't set up a chain of them at comfortable intervals, like oases on a map. Finding them is the job of the shepherd, not of the sheep. When they come, they are serendipities, unexpected blessings. I think it is not accidental that the Psalm says, "He *makes* me to lie down in green pastures." Some translations put it, "He lets me . . . ," which misses the point, I think. Some green pastures I don't even recognize. Sometimes when my soul is being restored, I fret at the inactivity which itself seems like an interruption.

But in my pilgrimage, I have happily discovered that life is not ever and eternally an uphill climb. At selected times and places, God has stopped me at a plateau and I had time to admire the view, even noting some progress. Then, in God's own time and in his own way, the journey continued.

If I could edit the Psalm by adding one line to "He maketh me to lie down," it would be, "He maketh me then to get up and go on." The greenest of pastures don't stay that way. They get overgrazed. Drought comes. They turn sere and brown.

We need green pastures as waystops. They provide refresh-
ment and strength. They are God's special blessings at unexpected intervals of the road. But the road goes on, and we
must go with it.

All the while binding up wounded fellow pilgrims, comforting distraught mothers, changing wet diapers.

Please don't keep your hands off

Something there is in the American life style that tends to communicate our preference for a "hands off" policy. If we had India's social system in this country, more than a few people would belong to the untouchable caste not because of social ostracism, but by a self-imposed isolation.

Football and hockey we happily term "contact sports," but probably only because 250-pound bodies in full-speed, head-on collision cannot be accused of gentleness. The South American *abrazo*, the male-to-male bear hug, has never become popular north of the border, even father-to-son. And lest you think it is only gruff Archie Bunker-types who strive to avoid touching, watch next Sunday when a latecomer edges into a pew ahead of you where others are already sitting. There may be ample space for all, but invariably the ones who were there first slide away from the newcomer. We may think we are being courteous, or that we are showing that we do not want to shut out anyone. But why wouldn't it make as much—or more—sense to edge toward the newcomer?

It looks suspiciously as if we are afraid to get too close. Or to allow anyone else to.

No doubt people as well as birds and animals have their

psychic space needs. A bird will let you approach just so near, and when you cross some invisible line that marks intrusion on his space, the bird will fly off. Wild animals react the same way. When a dog licks your hand, he is testifying not only to his adjustment to people generally but to his perception of your adjustment to him.

We are *so* hygienic, even when we are trying to care. If we put a quarter in an outstretched hand, we drop it from a safe, sterile distance. We don't press it down with finger contact— we might catch something. But compassion can't be produced by remote control and it won't survive long untouched by human hands.

I am convinced no one can truly help others from a "safe" distance. You cannot minister to someone to whose condition you cannot relate. I re-discovered that in an Egyptian garbage dump when I spent three days among the people who collect and recycle Cairo's refuse. Being with them—not only hearing about them—was important for them and for me. Real aid is never dispensed; it can only be shared. As Henri Nouwen, my currently favorite author, says in his book, *The Wounded Healer*, "The great illusion of leadership is to think that we can be led out of the desert by someone who has never been there."

Though Jesus did not always heal with a touch, he did it frequently. Sometimes it was touch at risk. There was the leper asking to be made clean whom Jesus touched. What a display of vulnerable love! No doubt Jesus could have cured the disease with only a word as he frequently did, which causes me to wonder if the touch wasn't meant to heal the man's emotions and spirit. No one had touched him since the first spot of leprosy appeared on his body. He had to call out "Unclean!" as others approached so they could be forewarned. Then along came this Man whose touch restored his sense of value and self-worth.

Many other stories in the Gospels show that not only did Jesus refuse to live by a hands-off policy, but he allowed others to touch him. In at least one instance, as many as touched the fringe of his garment were made well (Matt. 14:36). And there was the woman who had endured a flow of blood for twelve years. Mark wryly comments that she "had suffered much under many physicians, and had spent all she had, and was no better but rather grew worse." Her anonymity protected by the crowd, she came up behind Jesus and "touched his garment" (Mark 5:25–29). Immediately the hemorrhage ceased. She was healed as she touched him.

But something else significant also happened. When the woman was healed, Jesus knew that "virtue had gone out of him." The healing caused a loss of spiritual energy to the healer. It always does. (Which is one thing that troubles me about so-called "faith healers" who can touch scores and hundreds of people in the space of an hour or two and still bounce off the stage smiling.)

This cost in "virtue" or spiritual energy expended may be one reason why we try hard to keep everything hygienic, hands and hearts off; healing takes too much out of us. We cannot heal others without feeling their pain. Playwright Thornton Wilder has the angel rightly telling the paralytic man by the Pool of Bethesda, "In love's service, only the wounded can serve."

Psychiatrists who know how to empathize (it is important to make the distinction) have discovered that a strange transfer of pain and symptoms can take place from patient to physician. Burdens cannot simply be cut loose; they must be lifted free by caring hands. In healing, whether of bodies or minds, one cannot do anything significant without a "hands on" attitude.

Though a certain professional detachment enables doctor or pastor or social worker to deal with suffering, it is tragic for both parties when the doctor cannot hurt, the pastor cannot weep or the social worker cannot feel. It is the hurting, the weeping, the feeling that does at least part of the healing. Perhaps the larger part.

Where there is hurting—and that is everywhere—there is need for touching.

The wife of an associate of mine was visiting a nursing home with a group of carol singers. On the "disturbed" floor, she paused to take the hand of an elderly woman and hold it while she talked gently about Christmas, about the woman's neat appearance, about anything and everything. The woman could not talk, but with effort she slowly lifted to her lips the hand that held hers.

"She bit you!" the group leader said in dismay.

"No," my friend's wife replied, tears in her eyes. "She kissed me."

There *is* healing in a touch. Healing on both sides. Please don't keep your hands off.

Let's all rise from our seats

The other day while reading about a certain church, I came upon the fact that it "seats 900." That's a common enough way of describing size. The Houston Astrodome seats 50,000, the Los Angeles Memorial Coliseum, 91,000. But I wondered, is *seating* power the way a church should be measured? Wouldn't *sending* power be more relevant? I'd like to know if that church *sends* 900. Or even nine.

Perhaps we've fallen into the habit of lumping churchgoing with spectator sports, where it is the coming and not the going that is important. That may help to explain why we attach such importance to glossy, fast-paced church services in which even ushers are expected to perform with the choreographed precision of the Rockettes.

The entertainment industry knows all about slickness and image, and if we are trying only to fill seats, that's probably the route. But it seems to me that the church might better be trying to empty its seats. The church is, or ought to be, a sending agency. A recruiting office, as nearly as I can tell, doesn't talk about the number of recruits it can hold, but the number it has enrolled and sent. Come to think of it, I have never seen a very big or a very plush recruiting office. They

41

don't have to be, because the action is somewhere else.

Churches are not alone in their sedentary terminology. In a university, there is a chair of economics or history or whatever. A candidate wins or loses a seat in Congress. A judge sits. The word "see" in Holy See comes from the Latin word for seat. A committee has a chairman or, if you prefer, a chairperson. An inquiry in a meeting is addressed to the chair. We all seem to be preoccupied with sitting.

The particular posture is generally regarded as one of the better possibilities for relaxed noninvolvement, but for the Christian, sitting has perils.

The first Psalm opens with these words: "Blessed (or happy) is the man that walks not in the counsel of the wicked, nor stands in the way of sinners, nor sits in the seat of scoffers." That is an interesting downward progression—walking, standing, sitting. The last one, which takes the least energy and application, is the ideal posture, it would seem, for scorning.

Have you noticed that doers are not generally scorners? People who are busy don't have time or energy for faultfinding. That preoccupation is usually connected with idle hands and an idle mind.

Scoffing (or scorning) is mentioned in the same breath with walking in the counsel of the ungodly and standing in the way of sinners—or, as the Living Bible has it, following evil men's advice and hanging around with sinners.

In other words, if you are a scorner, that's the league you're playing in, even though scorning, as practiced by the Christian, is generally regarded as something less than full-blown, front-page sinning. It's a genteel, widely practiced, almost respectable sin, as we have come to grade sins. But it will subtract from your happiness just as surely and totally as will following evil men's advice and hanging around with sinners, according to the psalmist.

So beware. Sins of the tongue do not require agility or even mobility. A chair will do.

Fortunately, there are some chairs—wheelchairs among them—that scorners could never own. Here, heaven has come close to earth and earth to heaven. True, a physical handicap is no guarantee of sainthood, but from countless such seats of enforced immobility have come prayer and power that changed the world. My own prayer is that when a chair begins to look more inviting to me than it does right now, may God help me to make it a center of intercession and encouragement rather than of carping and criticism.

Resting can also be a redemptive use of a chair, especially if it means the restoration of strength for even more vigorous activity—as in the case of a time-out during a fast-paced basketball game. I don't know if God sat down when he finished his six days of creative work, but the book of Genesis says he rested, and that implies sitting.

Whatever the posture, times of inactivity should not be wasted time. Isaiah 40:31 indicates they can be used creatively by making God part of the time-outs: "They that wait upon the Lord shall renew their strength. They shall mount up with wings like eagles; they shall run and not be weary; they shall walk and not faint."

Just don't sit and wait too long; wings and feet may be readier than you think.

The prophet Ezekiel sat down redemptively, too. When he arrived among the exiles in Babylon, he was "in bitterness and in the heat of my spirit." But the angry and frustrated prophet says that for seven days "I sat where they sat" (Ezek. 3:14–15 KJV). As he began to feel the anguish and heartache of the refugees, his own bitterness gradually ebbed away and his spirit was healed.

Ezekiel found wholeness for himself when he spent some creative time in the chair of empathy for others.

But soon the voice of God said to him, "Arise!" The time comes when we need to get moving. Whenever it does, let's all rise from our seats.

And, like the prophet, go forth.

It's not safe to play it safe

They call it social *security*.

But the retirement assistance program seems so fragile that those who benefit from it, and those who hope to, wonder just how much security it actually represents. No different, really, from a lot of other supposedly secure things.

In these days when all foundations are being shaken, security is a word universally, longingly and mistakenly cherished. Universally because everyone wants it. Longingly because practically no one has it. Mistakenly because you don't get it by going after it—any more than happiness is achieved by hot pursuit (apologies to the drafters of the Declaration of Independence).

Mostly we hold a distorted view of security, a view which Jesus tries to straighten out. He says it's not safe to play it safe, or to use his own words, "Whosoever will save his life shall lose it," or in a modern version, "Anyone who keeps his life for himself shall lose it" (Matt. 16:25 LB). It must be a very important principle, because it appears four times in the gospels, twice in Matthew.

Many of us, however, are still not wholly convinced that it's a sound, workable, life-saving policy. It staggers our intellect to believe that security comes as a result of giving rather than getting; by risking rather than protecting what you have; by building bridges instead of fences; by opening windows rather than closing doors.

I don't know when I finally became convinced of that. Maybe I was like the White Queen whom Alice met in *Through the Looking Glass* who resolved to believe six impossible things every morning before breakfast. But I have a feeling it started the day I was reading Jesus' commission to his disciples in Matthew 10:16, "Behold, I send you out as sheep in the midst of wolves . . . " The Holy Spirit abruptly stopped me. It was a startling statement and the implications alarmed me.

Here was a plain, unvarnished warning of danger.

I agonized over that verse for weeks, often reminding the Lord how dangerous and deadly wolves are and how helpless and defenseless sheep are.

During this period of inner tension, I awakened very early one morning. Contrary to my usual frustrated behavior on sleepless nights, I quietly asked the Lord if he wanted to say something to me.

"Yes, Stan," I immediately sensed his answer. "You remember that verse you're troubled about?"

I remembered.

"The problem is," he continued, "you have been concentrating on the sheep instead of the Shepherd. You don't have to worry about your safety. The protection of the sheep is the responsibility of the Shepherd."

Fantastic! I decided then and there that I don't have to live; I only have to go with the Shepherd. My life took on a new cutting edge and ever since then I've been discovering an exhilarating boldness.

I don't claim complete success in getting my view of "saving and losing" straightened out. I do know that the closer I draw to the biblical priority, the more liberated, the "safer" I feel; and the farther away from that priority, the more insecure, the more worried, the more harried.

When I am about to leave for some far place of the earth, someone invariably asks, "Is it safe?" I want to retort, "It's not safe to be alive!" but my more courteous response is, "It's safe to be where I think God wants me to be, whether that is across the street or across the world."

Ted Agon, former operations chief of a refugee rescue vessel, *Seasweep*, which I organized in the late 1970s, has been involved with ships most of his life. Recently he sent me a motto which hangs on his wall. It says, "A ship in a harbor is safe, but that is not what ships are built for."

I love it. Ships at sea are battered by wind and wave, but they are built for the ocean. Harbor is a place to take on supplies, not a place to rust. Until a few years ago, scores of old World War II Liberty ships were anchored side by side in the Hudson River fifty miles north of New York. No danger of torpedo, mine or gale. Secure. Rusting. Useless.

Bible heroes and heroines, whose achievements in retrospect seem so predestined and easy, were always at risk. Do we think it was routine for Abraham to move on into a new country "not knowing whither he went"? Or that Moses had no second thoughts about moving out of Pharaoh's palace?

What made heroes then and makes them now is not superior intuition but a willingness to risk, by faith, for something beyond self-interest. Risk of itself is not particularly virtuous. Anybody can lose his life. The supreme tragedy is to lose one's life for nothing. Jesus says it counts only if it is "for my sake and the gospel's." That's why I want to die on company time while about my Father's business.

Charles A. Garfield, a West Coast professor, spent 15 years interviewing 1200 top performers in business, education, sports, health care and the arts to find out what made them achievers. Quoted in the *Wall Street Journal*, he said: "They avoid the so-called comfort zone. . . . They confidently take risks after laying out the worst consequences beforehand . . . . They set out the worst that can possibly happen and decide whether they can live with that outcome. If they can, they move ahead confidently. Other executives, when taking a risk, tend to be hampered by a sense of impending doom."

So I asked myself what is the "worst" that can possibly happen if I go with the Shepherd? The worst, it seems to me, is that in some new setting, some new experience, some new relationship, I will find adventure, growth and invigorating change.

That's losing my life? I can live with that!

It's not bad to feel good

There is no reason why doing good shouldn't feel good. Many of us have become so wary about good works ("lest any man should boast") that we do them out of a dull and compelling sense of duty, if, indeed, we do them at all. That way we are not allowed to take any credit or feel any joy.

Doing good works should be and can be joyful. God loves a cheerful giver (2 Cor. 9:7). I find no such promise for the cheerless giver, whose gift, while it may accomplish good, does not fill a void in his own life.

Granted, there are skilled manipulators—even well-intentioned ones—who get people to give by telling them how much they will get back or promising them recognition, instead of presenting the opportunity and letting the response arise from more worthy motivations. And certainly, giving can be ego-directed, if one gives simply to feel good or to get off one uncomfortable hook or another.

But some Christians seem so fearful that pride may infiltrate their good works (knowing that we don't and can't earn salvation), they minimize the danger by avoiding good works. They have not discovered the difference between taking pride and finding joy. There is the need of the receiver to receive and there is the need of the giver to give. Neither can stand alone. While doing one's best does not necessarily call for the creation of a new national holiday, knowing one has done it produces a measure of the joy that helps to make us whole persons.

There is a lot in the Bible about joy, including that strange verse which tells us to "consider it pure joy . . . whenever you face trials of many kinds" (James 1:2 NIV). The reason being, of course, that "the testing of your faith develops perseverance." It does no credit to God for a Christian to walk around with the look of terminal misery on his face.

Consider the verse on which I was brought up: "This is the day which the Lord hath made; we will rejoice and be glad in it" (Psalm 118:24 KJV). The word "rejoice" implies an act of the will—"be joyful." There is something positive about it. You don't sit there waiting for someone to suffuse you with joy. Rejoicing is something *you* do. "We *will* rejoice; we *will* be joyful."

And all this time we have been going on the basis that if it made you feel good, there was probably something wrong with it. The gospel is the Good News, not the bad news our cultivated cheerlessness would suggest. "Grin and bear it" is not a biblical admonition. We act as if, were we to let down our guard and be happy, we would tempt Satan to prove that life is a burden, not a celebration.

So lest we attract his attention, like Job, we keep a low happiness profile.

And the results are not merely neutral; they are negative. Suppressing the spontaneous joy which arises from doing good, we become susceptible to pride. (Being creatures of emotion, we cannot, after all, merely feel nothing.) The publican who went up to the temple and prayed ostentatiously was getting kicks from self-congratulations that he should have found in his otherwise exemplary life style. He was a methodical and even meticulous giver, but, clearly, he didn't get any fun out of his giving. Pride was all he had left.

Where is the balance between pride and joy? Jesus said, "When you give to the needy, do not announce it with trumpets, as the hypocrites do in the synagogues and on the streets, to be honored by men." (Besides, that way you'll get on a lot of mailing lists!) "I tell you, do not let your left hand know what your right hand is doing" (Matt. 6:3 NIV). But there is no reason why your right hand can't know what your right hand is doing. You don't have to hide your joy from yourself.

I received a letter from a troubled contributor struggling with some of these problems. "Because my husband and I give, and we generally give more than a tithe, we don't have new clothes or a T.V. like our friends, and we don't know if we'll ever be able to afford a home of our own. Materially we are 'poor' compared with all our friends. It is so hard to give when I don't get encouragement from those around me, and it's even harder when I wonder if God cares that I give. I wonder if God really cares about my 'works'? Does he care about my struggle to give? I guess I know deep inside that he cares and is pleased. But no one tells me that."

My observation is that knowing deep inside is knowing where it counts, but it is not unimportant to be aware that God cares. About Cornelius, the Bible says, "He and all his family were devout and God-fearing; he gave generously to those in need and prayed to God regularly. One day he . . . saw an angel of God, who came to him and said . . . 'Your prayers and gifts to the poor have come up as a remembrance before God'" (Acts 10:1–5 NIV).

God knew.

But even if heaven kept no record, the joy of doing something kind, something generous, is in the doing. In the knowing that good works are better than evil works. That love— even when it tears you to pieces—is better than aloofness. That the shared load somehow becomes more nourishing than the loaf unshared.

There is also the satisfaction of knowing that, because of

what one does, the blind who would not otherwise see receive sight, the lame who would not otherwise walk are made mobile, the deaf who would not otherwise hear are brought into the world of sound, the starving who would otherwise have died are alive, the homeless who otherwise would be unsheltered are housed, the naked who otherwise would be cold are clothed, and the Good News is preached to someone who otherwise would never have heard.

Giving is also a gift to the giver. Cheerfully (the word in the Bible literally means "hilariously") done, it brings him close to the heart of God.

And that's a good feeling.

Who do you think you are?

At a convention recently, a man walked up to a friend of mine, looked at his badge, and said, "Your name is familiar. What are you known for?"

When I heard the story, I decided it was a commentary on our times. My friend was not seen as someone who might be worth getting to know. His identity was connected to his notoriety, to image, to role.

More and more, Christians seem occupied with image. Obviously, corporations are. In the big ones, a gaggle of public relations experts constantly massage the image to make sure the company looks good. The objective is not necessarily that things *be* right; only that they *look* right.

There being no such thing as a corporate soul, that tactic is viewed merely as smart management. But for the Christian, it can be only a loser for if we are not real, we are nothing. Literally nothing, for image is only illusion. "What you see is what you get" is not true for believers, because reality is mostly behind what we are willing to let others see.

This self-deluding game makes relaxed living virtually impossible. We expend an enormous amount of time and emotional energy employing every kind of machination we know,

52

plus a few we invent, in order to project an idealized version of ourselves. We become emotional contortionists, twisting and squirming our way through techniques which include denial, repression, illusions, delusions, rationalization and deadening.

And all the while God leaves us free to be whatever we choose, real or unreal.

Finding out who you are is sometimes not easy and almost never comfortable. It requires looking within at our uncertainty, our insecurity, our low self-esteem. That is always more complicated and painful than gazing only at the untroubled, placid surface.

So we change the arena. Instead of exploring the inner spirit we phrase questions that focus on externals, like, "What do you do?" Inadequate as it is, activity then becomes the yardstick by which we measure worth.

The elders of a church, receiving a class of new members, asked each candidate to tell something about himself. One man spoke of his career achievements, his club memberships, the honors bestowed upon him. The group smiled its approval. He had told about himself. Then it was the turn of a woman who had come to faith out of atheism and alcoholism. She shared something of her spiritual pilgrimage.

"I'm so grateful that my struggle has brought me to this point of healing," she concluded. "I've come so far to get here."

"But tell us about *you*," one of the group insisted.

Eyes filling with tears of joy, she said, "That *is* me."

Which reminds me of what Jesus told the Pharisees, "I know where I came from and where I am going" (John 8:14 LB).

Blessed, confident and serene is the person who has such a sure fix on his or her identity.

In the church, we seem to go out of our way to cloak or sublimate personhood. Church leaders refer to members as "giving units." Others report new believers as "baptisms."

Evangelistic meetings result in card-signing "decisions for Christ." I'm not nearly as much concerned about what happened to the human race, a subject explored in a Christian film, as I am about what happened to persons! As for me, I want to be a flesh-and-blood human being, not a giving unit, a baptism, or even a decision for Christ.

If we ourselves are guilty of so diminishing the crown jewels of God's creation, how can we complain when the government turns each unique soul into an eleven-digit computer number?

The reason so many retirees fall apart is that they have been conditioned to think of life as a job resumé. Their identity is in what they have done and when the job goes, the identity goes. It is even worse for one who loses his job. As *Time* magazine puts it, "If joblessness goes on for long, men and women of all ages, occupations and economic classes tend to suffer a sharp loss of self-esteem, a diminished sense of identity, a sense of estrangement."

Even eulogies major in what the person did more than what he or she was. At one funeral, those present were invited to say something about the deceased. After a long, embarrassing pause, one man got up and said, "Clem could whistle *Yankee Doodle Dandy* better than anybody I know."

That wouldn't have counted in a Marxist society where people have value only as economic producers, but I believe it's O.K. in the kingdom of God. Jesus said, "Not one sparrow can fall to the ground without your Father knowing it," and sparrows can't even whistle.

The children and spouse of a person in the public eye carry their own burdens of identity. One of my daughters attended a Christian school where she was regularly introduced as "Stan Mooneyham's daughter." Pushing aside this stifling blanket of nonpersonhood, she always responded by saying, "My name is Gwen."

But often we impose our own masks. Afraid that people may not like us for ourselves, we cover our identity with some title or relationship. So our real self goes through life hidden, fearful, sweating behind the mask. It waits there, cringing in confusion, fear and aloneness, crying for discovery. But that self can't emerge until it is in a place of love, security and acceptance.

To be emotionally whole, each of us must sooner or later seek such a place. Much healing would happen if churches and small groups would allow themselves to *be* such a place.

For me, I have decided not to invent myself over again to fit the designs of others. I am me, and whatever I do for the rest of my life, it will be not in order to have an identity, but as a result of allowing my real self to emerge.

It's scary—but so, so satisfying.

Nor things to come

Pessimism may be the psychological plague of the late twentieth century—and Christian believers have found that not even faith provides immunity. Some of the most successful books on the evangelical market have been cheerless previews of the apocalypse. Even the title of a film about the Vietnam war played on the theme.

I have met young people immobilized by fear of the future. Nothing seems worth doing, because the world may fall apart in the middle of the doing. A sincere Christian couple told me recently, "We're not going to have children. We don't want to bring them into a world that may self-destruct."

Authors are building financial security for themselves by selling uncertainty to others. Just count the gloomy doomsday titles on the next rack of Christian paperback books you see. Preachers' doleful predictions of things to come, though well-intentioned, are not only scaring "hell" out of unbelievers, but heaven out of believers. Christians are more shaken than they have any right to be. Faith equates with confidence, not fear. Scripture does not authorize Christians to cringe or cower.

For one thing, there is no storm-proof shelter that offers

physical security and no ultimate economic shelter on this earth. Where would you take cover to escape apocalypse?

For another, there is the magnificent conclusion of Romans 8. You remember how Paul said it:

For I am persuaded, that neither death, nor life, nor angels, nor principalities, nor powers, nor things present, nor things to come . . . shall be able to separate us from the love of God, which is in Christ Jesus our Lord (vv. 38,39 KJV).

This passage has always been a favorite of mine—a shelter in the time of storm, a beacon in darkness, an encouragement in despair. But only recently I rediscovered what I think is one of its most important and most neglected phrases.

Nor things to come.

This is not something to be read only at funerals. It means things to come at any time. After death? Sure. But before death, too. Things like an energy shortage. Inflation. Recession. International turmoil. The feeling we're being outnumbered by lawbreakers, domestic and international. Things that happen in Washington, Moscow, Teheran, Riyadh, wherever. Things that happen on our own street, in our own family, on our own job.

Nor things to come.

Words to be written over our fears! Emblazoned over the lintel of tomorrow! Embedded in our hopes!

Things to come, whatever they may be, hold no paralyzing terror for those whose Lord is Christ Jesus. God's love does not come and go. He will not let anything get in its way.

Which means getting back to our Father's business-as-usual. Living with an unquenchable confidence, not so much knowing what or when or where, as Who. Not being utterly wiped out if the temperature goes as high as 78 or as low as 65—or if we have to make substantial adjustments in our way of living.

The sin in fear is that it causes us to hold back, to hoard our talents or resources or life itself. It is the enemy of sharing, cautioning us to hold on to that crust of bread rather than to cast it on the waters.

Too risky, fear says.

But faith says, *"Nor things to come."*

Four little words that restore our perspective, cool our feverish self-centeredness, unclench our fists, straighten our backs, get us going again.

Nor things to come.

Always it is the future that we worry about most. Things present we somehow cope with, however distressing. Nine-tenths of fear hides in the future tense. Fear lives not in the known, but in the unknown. Not in what is already here but in what hasn't yet arrived. But see: "Neither . . . things present, *nor* things to come."

Faith is always for the unexplored place, the experience we have not yet had. "A man who already has something doesn't need to hope and trust that he will get it" (Rom. 8:24 LB). Or not get it. Faith is the force that starts our blood circulating, our juices flowing, our thoughts and feet and hands moving. Abraham "went out, not knowing whither he went." What he did know was with Whom he went. That was enough.

From Genesis to Revelation, the good word is, "Fear not."

Neither things present.

Nor things to come.

That doesn't turn a Christian into a twittering Pollyanna. But it should make one an unwavering optimist. It's the believer's birthright.

Faith and freeze-dried food

On the wall of my local Sloppy Joe's where I sometimes go for a noontime sandwich, there used to hang this bit of wry humor: "If you can keep your head while all about are losing theirs, you just don't know how serious the situation is." Purveyors of doomsday panic, who apparently have discovered a lucrative market among readers of evangelical magazines, would like us to believe this modified version: "If you can keep your faith while all about are losing theirs, you don't know how bad things are."

According to certain fair-weather believers, faith is okay when such really important issues as income or survival are not at stake; but if your real-life, concrete situations start to deteriorate, you'd best opt for the highest interest rate or its equivalent.

I know it doesn't sound very pious when you say it straight out like that, but it's an easy impression to get from the way choices are made, even by Christians. We want a risk-free faith; that's why we signed up for the heavenly insurance policy which gives us a piece of the Rock of Ages.

The notion seems to be that there are two worlds—the "real" world where we live as citizens, and the "make-believe" world where we live as Christians. In a crunch, the "real" world is the one that usually takes priority.

That misdirected priority is nowhere more evident than in the survivalist mood abroad in the land, becoming big enough to be noticed by the news media. Writing in the *New York Times*, Flora Lewis says, "There are now thousands of people preparing doomsday hideaways and learning to shoot so they won't have to share with neighbors." She cites some research done by my friend and Associated Press correspondent, Peter Arnett, who in a dozen states found people "spending huge sums to pile up caches of freeze-dried food, medicine and ammunition against the day of dog-eat-dog rule in the United States."

One woman in Georgia told Arnett, "We are not just concerned about nuclear war. What if we have a serious tornado? We still need to protect ourselves from others."

We are not told about the religious faith of these survivalists. My guess is that many of them are regular churchgoers. Probably they are professed Bible-believers, although they seem to have no confidence in God's department of defense. Where God is weak, they propose to be strong.

It all sounds so much like the Israelites who *believed* in God, but *trusted* in horses and chariots. Why is it that in situations where it can be measured in tangible terms, faith is so easily discardable?

Sunday Christians might do well to turn on Monday morning to 1 John 3:17ff: "If anyone has material possessions and sees his brother in need but has no pity on him, how can the love of God be in him?" (NIV). The next verse also relates: "My children, love must not be a matter of words or talk; it must be genuine and show itself in action" (NEB). And the next: "This then is how we know that we belong to the truth" (NIV).

This then is how we know!

There are so many *this thens* waiting for acts of testimony, acts which sometimes may be at risk, acts that find and are found by the "test" in testimony.

It doesn't say that when we're doing fine, thank you—no community or world problems, no heartache, no inflation, no tornadoes or nuclear threat, no hungry people pounding at the door or facing us on the television screen—*this then* is how we know that we belong to the truth. No such qualifiers are given.

But in spite of that idealism about the meek, doesn't life really belong to the strong, the provident, the foresighted, the full-pantried, the well-armed? Apparently not for very long, if one man's experience means anything. The Lord said to him, "This night thy soul shall be required of thee" (Luke 12:20 KJV).

"If anyone has . . . and sees his brother in need but has no pity . . . ." Which brings us to the last desperate defense of the Christian cowering behind barricades: "But he's not my brother!" You'd best accept the judgment of a higher court regarding that. Jesus said, "Whoever does the will of God is my brother" (Matt. 12:50). As the hymn puts it, "Who loves my Father as a son is surely kin to me."

Times are coming—you can count on it—when it will be easy to put first things second, when being Christian in action will seem the most illogical, irrelevant response you can make as the so-called real world around you starts to crumble.

When that happens, those who belong to the truth will keep the faith. They are the ones who not only know how bad things are; they also know how completely dependable God is.

It is no casual promise Jesus makes: "Lo, I am with you alway, even unto the end of the world" (Matt. 28:20 KJV).

"Those are the words of a gentleman," David Livingstone said, "given on his sacred honor."

Some thoughts about the bandwagon

For decades evangelicals were at the bottom of the American political power structure. If anyone in government wondered what evangelicals thought about the issues—which he rarely did—it was after policy had already been set. If the words "born again" had been uttered during a television interview, the embarrassed host would have steered the conversation to safer ground. If the term came up in a newspaper story, the reporter or editor carefully explained in parentheses: "The expression 'born again' appears in a conversation between Jesus and Nicodemus that may be found in chapter 3, verse 3 of the Gospel according to St. John, one of the books of the New Testament."

Then, almost overnight, evangelicals were discovered. *Publishers Weekly*, prestigious trade journal of the book industry, announced with no little amazement that religious titles, including *The Living Bible*, were among the best of the bestsellers. They had been all along, of course, but because they were primarily sold in evangelical bookstores, there was no input to the bestseller measuring mechanism. More bestsellers appeared, written by political, sports and stage personalities who recounted their dramatic conversion (and sometimes pre-conversion) experiences.

Evangelical television shows began competing handily with secular programs. Evangelicals were buying not only radio and television *time*, but radio and television *stations*. On the drawing boards were networks and communications satellites.

Instead of being a handicap, a confession of Christian faith was regarded by many as being a downright political asset.

Evangelicalism, leaping over denominational fences to form a new and biblical ecumenism, has become a force to be reckoned with politically, ecclesiastically, socially, and conversationally. Evangelicals are suddenly newsworthy. They are listened to, cultivated, cajoled, wheedled, subsidized and at times exploited.

Evangelical followers of Christ now have a bandwagon on which to carry their cross.

Popularity is a heady experience. To be respected is more fun than to be ignored. It's a lot nicer to be a somebody than a nobody. One is also better able to do good with power than without it.

And yet . . .

God has so seldom used the wise to confound the foolish, and has so often used the foolish to confound the wise—probably because the wise so regularly cease to be usable.

He more often uses the weak than the strong, the powerless than the powerful, the meek than the mighty, the humble than the proud. In the midst of our splendor, can we really believe that it is "not by might, nor by power, but by my Spirit"? Perhaps—but only with great difficulty.

The trouble with basking in bigness and rejoicing in respectability is that we begin to believe it is the normal Christian condition. It is not impossible to imagine that someday we will have a truly "popular" paraphrase of the Scriptures which might render Matthew 5:11 in this way: "When men shall praise you and say all manner of good about you for your ego's sake, rejoice and be exceeding glad, for that is your great reward. If the prophets before you hadn't been so obstreperous, they, too, would have been applauded." If this reversed vision were read from the pulpit some Sunday morning, there might not be so much as a double-take.

The thought which nags me is that evangelical popularity reacts to and depends upon the same values and measures that apply to everyone and everything else. The success syndrome causes us to forget that only God can measure success. Because he measures with the yardstick of eternity, Jesus shocks us with these words: "What sadness is ahead for those praised by the crowds" (Luke 6:26 LB).

None of which, it should be pointed out, demands of the true believer that he be cantankerous, contrary to the apparent conviction of some. The authentic prophet does not offend people in order to authenticate his prophecy. He simply calls the plays as, enlightened by the Holy Spirit, he sees them. He attempts neither to be popular nor to be unpopular, only to be faithful to the Word of the Lord. It is not necessary to work consciously at being unpopular. That comes easily enough. One need only be honest in a dishonest world, truthful in a deceitful world, peaceful in a warring world, loving in a hating world, selfless in a selfish world, compassionate in a ruthless world.

Our measure will not ultimately be taken by how many battalions or votes or celebrities or newspaper headlines we can field. Not even a *Time* cover story will add points. The divine scoring system is based only on faithfulness. God will take our little or our much and make of it what he wishes— just so long as we do not think we have so little that he does not need us, or so much that we do not need him.

United we fall

The increasing use of evangelical power in the political arena seems to stand a good chance of being the issue—replacing inerrancy—most likely to divide evangelicals in this decade.

Personalities and issues arising in election years provide the most visible demonstration of the use of this power, especially if the contests can be portrayed as good vs. evil or moral vs. immoral. But more subtle is the formation of power blocs and mailing lists to be called up at any time to give support to what is declared to be a "Christian" political position, whether it is on abortion or nuclear disarmament.

Evangelicals, who are growing in numbers and strength to majority status, are sensing their clout. Television and the media have provided loyal and massive audiences for a number of Christian leaders. The names of some of them have become household words. There appears to be an increasing feeling that it would be a shame not to use just a little of all that accumulated popularity and influence for political purposes.

The strange thing about this is that less than two decades ago religious conservatives were scathingly critical of religious liberals who were political activists. One even wonders what it might be like if, say a decade from now, the

Roman Catholics produced another spellbinding television preacher—like the late Fulton Sheen—who used his charisma and mailing list to recruit national support for federal aid to parochial schools and against artificial methods of birth control? Certainly in the old days when the "liberal" National Council of Churches issued a statement that had political overtones—as it frequently did—embarrassed conservatives in and out of the Council's constituency rushed to say, "They don't speak for me!"

Public pronouncements by clergymen, denominations and ecumenical committees were regularly denounced and disowned. Now one wonders if evangelicals are little more than liberals-come-lately!

Political power has long been recognized as a seductive, secular temptation. It also must be seen as a seductive religious temptation. It requires no biblical language expert to paraphrase into our modern evangelical mood the words of Israel in 1 Samuel 8:19: "We will have a king over us, that we also may be like all the nations." Simply substitute "President . . . congressman . . . senator . . . governor" for king, and translate "all the nations" into "power blocs."

I sense that is the growing mood of some of my fellow evangelicals, and it scares the daylights out of me. The Israelites discovered after they got what they wanted that power, even with anointed beginnings, has an unfortunate way of turning in upon and magnifying itself. I see little to convince me that evangelical power—past or present—is less immune to that kind of misuse than any other kind of power.

Failure to adopt a hardline political position—right or left—and to mobilize behind the appropriate issue or candidate seems to have become the evangelical cardinal sin. In a recent election year I alienated friends on both sides by declining invitations to endorse their respective positions. It is no longer enough, I have learned, to support a candidate who is simply a Christian. He or she must also carry the appropriate modifier, *liberal* or *conservative*.

Fragmentation is sure to occur as support of a particular political cause or candidate becomes more the litmus test of

Christian authenticity than the Apostles' Creed. Surely Jesus' prayer for his disciples and us that we might all be one didn't necessarily mean that we have to pull the same voting machine lever.

There is a subtle but real danger in this grasp for Christian power and influence, not only for those of us who are being pushed but for those doing the pushing (and who presumably earn prestige points, and maybe more, if their candidate wins). During the temptation in the wilderness, the devil, playing kingmaker, offered Jesus "all the kingdoms of the world and the glory of them." I used to think this temptation to raw power left Jesus cold. But maybe not. Maybe he was tempted to rationalize a positive answer in the same way that some of his followers today can make it all sound so reasonable and right.

One difference between then and now is that Jesus recognized who the tempter was.

I am as frightened of an evangelical power bloc as I am of any other. Worldly power in religious hands—Islamic or Christian—has hardened into more than one inquisition. That God has delivered us from the hands of zealous, but misguided, saints is all that at times has saved us.

Although it is not impossible to harmonize the two in some situations, there is actually a basic conflict between Christian commitment and political power. The strength of faith is in its avalanche of powerlessness, its tidal force of love. If politics is the art of achieving the possible, faith is the art of achieving the impossible. Politics says, "Destroy your enemies." Christian faith says, "Love your enemies." Politics says, "The end justifies the means." Christian faith says, "The means validate the end." Politics says, "The first shall be first." Christian faith says, "The last shall be first."

I shall certainly continue to participate in the political process, and I hope you will. I will vote with care and a sense of responsibility, and I believe you will. That is all that either of us has the right, as Christians, to request of the other.

And when I go to church, I expect to be looking up at the pulpit for a pastor, teacher, friend. Not for a ward-heeler.

Birth, babyhood and ballyhoo

How disorientingly fast things change.

Take, for example, "born again."

Once limited to the language of revivals and camp meetings, the expression is now used freely and without apology almost everywhere. The term is so "in" that most polls on religious and moral issues have provided a category for born-again believers. The strategies of Madison Avenue and Hollywood indicate that that they, too, recognize the significant share of the marketplace occupied by people who admit to having been born again.

Though I can find "born again" only three times in the New Testament, the metaphor is a particularly apt one, describing as it does the complete newness that the beginning Christian encounters. How can that newness be explained? What is it like? It is like, well, being suddenly launched into a new world. It is like ... becoming a new person. It is like ... being born again!

But watch out. It's a tricky little analogy that implies an awful lot of things not normally thought about when the phrase is carelessly thrown around.

For example, newborn infants are not expected to announce their arrival on the scene in very articulate ways. No one expected a Gettysburg Address from the infant Lincoln or St. Augustine to write his *Confessions* as a child. How amazing it is, then, that we seem to expect baby Christians to arrive on the scene endowed with the wisdom of Solomon, the silver tongue of William Jennings Bryan and the theological insights of Luther and Calvin. The first week we push them before a class of teenagers, and onto an evangelical convention platform the week after that.

Is it reasonable to expect a newly converted drug dealer or porno star to start talking like one of the Puritan fathers the week after an announced conversion?

My plea is: Let the newborn have their babyhood! After Saul of Tarsus was converted on the Damascus road, he spent three years in an Arabian desert before he attempted to verbalize what had happened to him. Somewhere out of the public eye is not a bad place for a new Christian to spend his babyhood. It's better to let him have a private place where he can spit up his milk and soil his diapers before asking him to perform for our friends.

Did you ever stop to think that when a baby is born, it isn't so much the baby who knows what happened as it is those around him? The mother certainly knows. The doctors and nurses know. The grandparents know. The neighbors soon know.

But the baby is still just a bundle of uncomprehending nerve cells. When the newborn leaves the hospital, he doesn't know he has come home. But the family knows. How the family knows! There's the crying. And the feedings—the bathings—the changings—the disruption of routines. They know by all the activities of love and caring which witness that a baby has been born.

See how tricky the metaphor is? Shouldn't the lives of those nearby be noticeably touched when a member of the family or business circle is born again? In fact, shouldn't the difference be so visible, so recognizable that the good news is spread by the witnesses?

Good news like: "Things are certainly different around here

since Bill became a Christian," and "It's a happier home since Mary Beth was born again," and "You just wouldn't know the old shop since Harry became a new person."

After that comes the growing up, the maturing. This, too, is visible and measurable, like the penciled growth marks on a door jamb. Growth is evidenced as the maturing Christian begins to transfer interest from self to others. Babies are concerned only with their own needs and comforts. They cry for no one except themselves. The orientation of their lives around "me" and "my" is total.

But Paul advises those who are growing up to "put away childish things." When "me" and "my" are replaced by "us" and "our," we are beginning to think like spiritual adults. When we cry for others and hurt with others, we are growing up. But the Christian who still thinks only of himself, prays only for his own needs, praises only for his own blessings, cannot be far from his spiritual womb.

Above the born-again ballyhoo, I'd like to hear some clear voices speaking about discipleship, growth in grace and maturity. Much as we cherish our infants and sometimes sentimentally wish they could stay small and cuddly, one of the most poignant of parental heartbreaks is the child who forever remains a child.

Does God have that heartbreak so much of the time with so many of us? And some of the time with all of us?

Discipling—more than meets the ear

You can say one thing about the modern Christian vocabulary. It is colorful. We keep adding all those exotic Greek words—*kerygma, koinonia, diakonia*—as if *gospel, fellowship* and *service* were somehow inadequate.

Action words are also big. "Thrust" is still having its day. No one ever has just an evangelistic effort anymore; it's always an evangelistic thrust. But then one day I heard one of those "thrusts" being referred to as an "evangelistic invasion." At that I wondered if we had started beating our pruning hooks into spears and our plowshares into swords, even before we had learned how to do it the other way around.

I'm disturbed by another fad word—"discipling," or, in the infinitive form, "to disciple." We all know about disciples, for they were people who followed Jesus, but suddenly the noun has become a verb and we are urged to go out and disciple people. Never mind that in the Great Commission we are told to "make disciples," which places the emphasis on the learning process. That's what "disciple" means—a learner. We have shifted the emphasis away from the learner to the teacher, as in "become a discipler."

Brand new converts are being told, "Find someone to disci-

ple," and they are urged to enroll in discipling seminars. It
has become a fad word, an easy word, even an egotistical
word.

And I don't like it.

It's a fad because we're forgetting what the word means.
It's easy because it implies little more than some quick in-
and-out preachments. It smacks of egotism for it seems to say,
"Sit down and I will teach you all you need to know about the
Christian life."

Sometime ago I was at a retreat for college-age young people. They were being exhorted by their leaders to "disciple
someone." Feeling that this was a responsibility not to be
taken on oneself casually and lightly, I sounded a note of
caution, reminding them of James' words: "My brothers, not
many of you should become teachers, for you may be certain
that we who teach shall ourselves be judged with greater
strictness" (James 3:1 NEB).

While some more mature Christians may indeed be gifted
and called to teach, even teachers need to continue to be
learners. After all, to "disciple" someone else—if such a word
makes semantic sense—is to be learners together.

How much better it would be, I said, if we approached
someone with the confession, "Friend, I'm a pilgrim, too. Can
we walk together and help each other? There is so much more
I need to know."

I can honestly say I have never met a woman or man or
child from whom I couldn't learn something. Some of my best
learning has been done in some of the most out-of-the-way
places among the most so-called primitive peoples. I'm not
talking about learning how to weave baskets of bamboo or
build a house of logs and bark and vines. I don't really have
need for those skills.

I'm talking about learning how to live without air condi-
tioning, color television, running water, supermarkets and all
the rest which have become our essentials. Learning how to
cope with poverty, hunger, disaster and early death. Learning
how to receive when you have nothing to give.

Those are the hard lessons which I have great need to learn.

As my respect grew for their family loyalty, their battered aspirations, their spiritual reaching, so opened the channel through which I could share my own spiritual reachings and findings. Because I love them, I could tell them about the Savior who loves them. These people were not my pupils. They were not my chore for the day nor even my good deed for the day. They were my fellow strugglers, my fellow learners.

I have seen more character in the faces of some men in breechcloths than I have seen in the faces of some church elders. In those sun-browned, wind-burned faces I have seen the same yearnings, the waiting friendliness, even the ready humor as that in the faces of my own compatriots. It has occurred to me that one of the troubles with a lot of our so-called "discipling" is that we don't take time to look into faces. We think we are the only ones with anything worth sharing, and that we can do it by rote or by writ.

In the story of the rich young ruler, there is an interesting progression. We are told in Mark 10, "Jesus beholding him loved him, and said unto him . . . ." The order is not insignificant. First, Jesus beheld him, then loved him, then spoke to him.

Often we get it backwards, figuring that saying is the place to start. Sometimes we follow our words with loving and occasionally with "beholding," but I fear that much of what passes for witnessing operates sight unseen, touch untouched and feelings unfelt.

As if it all took place in a vacuum.

Sad.

That is why I think one who has been a Christian six months or sixty years had better think twice and pray often before sitting someone down willy-nilly for discipling.

For a discipler is someone who not only teaches.

But who learns.

And looks.

And loves.

The affliction of adjectivitis

It's one of the most contagious diseases in Western Christendom, and there seems to be no stopping it. Perhaps inflation is to blame. As it takes more and more money to buy the same thing, so it seems to take more and more words to explain what we mean.

Some of that has been going on for a long time. As far back as Antioch, Christians were called Christians. As the church grew and changed, modifiers came into use. It got so that it was not enough to be a generic Christian—you had to be some particular brand-name Christian. Eventually the modifier became the important identification factor. You didn't say, "I'm a Methodist Christian. I'm a Baptist Christian." You said simply, "I'm a Methodist. I'm a Baptist." As in the case of the word "Christian," the modifiers were mostly pinned on by others. But we wore them.

That was bad enough in our own country where "conversion" might consist mainly of a switch of denominational labels rather than a change of nature. It was even worse on mission fields, where adjectival competition, baffling and destructive, must have evoked many mutters of "Why don't they go back where they came from until they get their act together?"

I can remember—it was not that many decades ago—when denominational brand-name fervor was of a heat that would put a nuclear meltdown to shame. Christians would fight each other at the drop of an adjective. Churches walled themselves away from each other by their modifiers. Then a new spirit started to catch hold. We began speaking to each other when we met on the street. We even had a few interdenominational services, especially at Thanksgiving and Easter. The sharp competitiveness faded.

Ecumenical movements—Christian Endeavor, the Student Christian Movement and others—helped our young people to get acquainted. Mutual friendships led to mutual respect. Church councils sprang up; they did a useful job, but were primarily associations of leaders, not followers.

The evangelical movement, when it came along, was born not only out of reaction against "liberalism" but out of the emergence of crossover fellowships at the grassroots. In some special sense, the great evangelical groupings were bottom-to-bottom and then bottom-to-top movements, rather than top-to-top and top-to-bottom. Their distinctiveness was in the word "evangelical," rooted in the biblical "evangel" or "good news." The good news was that Christ died for sinners, news that some churches were not reporting enthusiastically.

Then something happened among evangelicals. The adjectives got to us. As mistrust began to sprout, we heard not just about evangelicals but about "conservative evangelicals." To emphasize the rightful place of the Bible in Christian faith and doctrine, someone slipped in another modifier, "Bible-believing," to make sure *that* loophole was plugged (although almost no one was going around saying that he was a "Bible-nonbelieving evangelical"). Then the modifier "born-again" was added, receiving impetus a few years ago. So now we had "conservative, born-again, Bible-believing evangelicals."

But that's not all. "Real" and "genuine" have also been favorites, though not in the same creative league with, for example, "Christ-honoring." "Socially conscious" was a belated arrival to the list of modifiers, and "Spirit-filled" another. Put them together and so far we have "genuine, conservative, born-again, Bible-believing, Christ-honoring, socially conscious, Spirit-filled evangelicals."

And the end, undoubtedly, is not yet.

I think I am all of these. But for me, evangelical says it all. The more words we string together as modifiers, the more we downgrade the word which is modified. In fact, we are saying that "evangelical" doesn't mean anything until we say what it means—like the umpire who in an argument over a play at first base snapped, "It ain't nuthin' till I call it."

As I said, creeping adjectivitis is catching. We're even hearing about "true truth," which, I must confess, confuses me utterly. Will someone please tell me if there is such a thing as "untrue truth"? Either of these modifiers takes the heart out of rational communication and perhaps out of truth itself.

What can we do about it? As for me, I refuse to give in to modifiers to describe myself or others. I wish I could be just an ordinary, garden variety Christian. But I know that won't satisfy a lot of people who want to test my orthodoxy. So when there is need for a special label, I'd like to be able to use a certain New Testament expression which has been almost lost but which, in its pure state, contains a wealth of simple meaning—"follower of the Way." But even that has become the appropriated label of a particular group, and I would probably be misunderstood.

But here's what I really believe.

I believe that among Christ's followers it shouldn't be necessary to have a scorecard to tell who is what. Except the one that Jesus himself offered: "All men will know that you are my disciples if you love one another" (John 13:35 NIV).

But, of course, that's too easy.

And, perhaps, too hard.

Emotional cloning is never Christian

Much has been written about the tragedy of Guyana, but I think there is something more to be said—something that addresses not Jonestown but Ourtown. Something that speaks to the nature and quality of our commitments. To say that Jim Jones, the man who led his people to their deaths, had "changed" or become paranoid or was mentally and spiritually sick does not deal with the other 916 who died by their own hand or at the hands of others.

They, too, were sick—infected with the virus of misdirection, of surrender of the will in the wrong way to the wrong lord. It is a sickness which did not disappear with the collapse of the Jonestown utopian dream.

Christian discipleship is founded on the bedrock of commitment, but it goes wrong if and when privatism takes over and the checks and balances of the group—the Body—are not, or cannot be, brought to bear upon what may be for some a personal revelation and for others personal ambition. It is too easy for one person alone, without counselors, to sanctify almost any means to achieve what he is convinced is a good and noble end.

God does use individuals, and sometimes it seems that he

works best through those who persist in the face of strong opposition. But there comes a time when every Christian, the most powerless as well as the most powerful, must be measured by the Holy Spirit as he works through other Christians. And more than that, by the measuring rod of Scripture, rightly divided. There comes a time when private revelation must stand the test of public examination.

To have charisma enough to attract a following is not enough. Perhaps, indeed, we have let our notions of charisma get out of hand. A charism is a gift from God, conferred not as a merit badge but as an empowerment for us to do what God wants us to do. The charism is God's for God's purposes, and if otherwise used, it is misused. How often we wait for a charismatic Godot to stir us while disregarding less dramatic, but faithful leadership made available by God! Faithfulness is also a charism.

The Bible admonishes us to temper our commitment by testing the spirits. One test, it seems to me, is that an authentic call to commitment is never a call to the diminishing of personality, but is always a call to the enhancing of it. We are not called to blind, irrational obedience, but to open-eyed, cause-and-effect obedience. We have a right and responsibility to question any cause and/or leadership which tries negatively to alter personality and will to guarantee the obedience of their followers.

Whether it's the Moonies or Moral Majority.

Commitment and surrender, in the context of Christian faith, result neither in a destroyed will nor in a reduced intellect. Nor do they rob us of the power and privilege of responsible choice as does allegiance to a false shepherd. But with all that, there is still the mystique of faith, still the incredible power of love, that lead us above and beyond our human rationalities and make of us, as they did of Abraham, more than we have been, not less.

Emotional cloning is never Christian. The desired goal is not to reduce everyone to a common denominator personality, but to elevate everyone to a fully alive, fully contributing personality. The need is not to subdue personality but to Christianize it. Jesus didn't try to make twelve carbon copies out of the men he chose. The leader who diminishes his followers does not pass the test of truly caring for the sheep.

The practice of privatism among evangelicals has long bothered me. Why is it that zeal and ambition cause so many gifted leaders to disregard the counsel and opinions of other members of the Body, who, far from being competitive or threatening, are essential to the health of the very ones who scorn them? Charismatic personalities who refuse to seek and listen to the advice of a "multitude of counselors" (Prov. 11:14) are in serious danger of losing their bearings and direction.

Any part of the Body, if separated from every other part, soon becomes a gross distortion with inevitable nightmarish results—different from Jonestown only in degree—because the balance of relationship is lost.

Yet it is that kind of privatism in which some seem to glory—bits and pieces trying to live independently and in the end dying ignominiously.

"Not good if detached" is more than a warning on a train ticket. It speaks to every believer about the necessity of being related to the rest of Christ's Body. We must be willing to listen to each other, be counseled by each other, supplement and complement each other—not because it is courteous to do so, which it is, but because it is Christian.

Only in the Body are we safe. Fulfilled. And fulfilling. It may seem heroic and exhilarating to march to the beat of a different drummer, but it is safe only if the rhythm is not out of step with the rest of the Body in which we are all mutually related.

Jim Jones is no more, but the folly which did him in is still very much with us.

It's me, it's me, O Lord

When we evangelicals sing these words to confess we are "standing in the need of prayer," it is a personal and therapeutic admission. But today's concentration upon "me" has gone far beyond humility. We evangelicals these days seem to be interested not so much in confessing as in possessing. We have become too introspective for our own—or anybody else's—good.

Not many years ago Christians were distressed by the "Me Generation"—those people, mostly young, whose only concern was themselves. If it felt good, it was good (no matter how it made someone else feel). "What's in it for me?" was the one question worth asking.

After that era—and growing out of it—something called self-awareness came along. "Self-absorption" might be a better name for it. The idea was to look within oneself, be "open," be "natural," "let it all hang out," and then one would be "fulfilled" while anxieties and hangups would disappear. The experience itself was said to be more valuable than what it produced as a consequence. One of the key words was "interiorizing." Scores of self-help books, courses, and large and small groups emerged.

If all this had stayed in "the world"—the world which
Christians *expect* to be self-centered—there would be little
reason for surprise. But like so many trends, fads and foibles
that evangelicals tend to legitimize about twenty years later,
we gradually developed our own brand of me-ness.

Tune around the Christian radio dial and listen to what is
being offered. Watch religious television. Interiorizing is
going on all over the place. We are told how to be more successful, more powerful, better liked, how to make more money, how to cope with guilt, loneliness, divorce, singleness, ill
health, old age, middle age, youth. Look through the religious
magazines and see the books that are being advertised. Im-
mediacy and introspection predominate. Such books are advertised because that is what evangelicals are buying. We are
buying because it is what many of us are interested in. Listen
to our gospel songs; is "self-centered" too strong an
adjective?

We are well into our own Me Generation.

Of course it is unarguable that success is better than
failure—at least it feels better—but whose measuring stick
are we using and how long is it? Coping is better than not
coping, but we do not cope in a vacuum. No Christian is an
island. We are bound up with neighbors, as Jesus dramat-
ically made clear in the parable of the Good Samaritan. We
live in communities and nations and hemispheres and in a
world. I doubt that it is possible to cope individually or without considering those with whom we have relationships in
the body of Christ.

A tribe in East Africa may understand this better than most
of us. When the first greeting of the day is exchanged, one
person asks another, "Are you well?" The response is, "I am
well if you are." Among this group, individual well-being is
not possible apart from the wholeness of the community.

This seems to be closer to what Jesus taught than most of
what is being practiced by his followers today.

We're accepting the wrong things as evidence of achieve-

ment. "Faith is the evidence of things *not* seen." We have
become less inquisitive and more acquisitive. "Supposing
that gain is godliness," we aim for gain (1 Tim. 6:5 KJV).
Believing that someday we shall reign with him, many of us
are in no mood to wait. But a quick look at 2 Timothy 2:12
will tell us the correct order of events on that one: *"If we
suffer*, we shall also reign with him" (KJV).

Christ is passing out no kingships now, only crosses. Christ
teaches us how to give more, not how to get more; how to
suffer, not how to escape; the importance of sharing, not the
necessity for hoarding; how to be a servant, not how to demand special privilege; how to handle a towel, not a scepter.

In a sense, *"me"* is the place where things must begin: "Just
as *I* am, without one plea, but that Thy blood was shed for
me." But it shouldn't end there. How many times a day is it
necessary for us to check our spiritual blood pressure?

Me-ism is eloquently summarized in a television commercial featuring a famous sports personality, who was advertis-
ing a brand of vitamins. She could as well have been promot-
ing some of the current brands of evangelicalism when she
concluded her endorsement: ". . . because you can never do
enough for yourself."

Then there's Chester Bitterman, the Wycliffe translator
taken hostage in Colombia and murdered when his organization would not pay ransom for his release. Bernie May, Wycliffe's U.S. director, soliciting prayer for Chester shortly before his body was found, wrote: "Chet knew when he joined
Wycliffe that it was risky business. But following Christ is
always that—for all of us. It is mandatory as we move from
Gethsemane toward Calvary that we know who we are and
where we stand when the torches light the garden at
midnight."

When we can say, *"Use* me, Lord—use even me," that's a
Me Generation worth belonging to.

Praying in the plural

Los Angeles freeways, most residents agree, make up the finest highway system in the country. Unlike many other traffic arteries elsewhere, these are toll-free, perhaps because here the automobile is almost the sole means of transportation for local citizens.

Many-laned and well-marked, the freeways are only a little less crowded in off-peak hours than in rush hours. Ingenious and complicated interchanges allow traffic to move smoothly from one freeway to another, and one of them near the heart of Los Angeles—a veritable Colossus of Roads—is often pictured when some national magazine wants to symbolize motor transportation. The freeways provide probably the best ground travel method anywhere for covering long distances in a hurry.

And yet all it takes to bring that flow of traffic to a sudden halt is one disabled car. Let one car have to stop and in seconds the freeway becomes, in the words of one longsuffering commuter, "the longest parking lot in the world." Even when the obstacle is removed, it may be hours before the traffic regains its pace. It amazes me that all this can be caused by something as simple as four lanes having to squeeze into three.

83

The other day when I was caught in one of these jams, I began to think about prayer. For, like many of you, I pray when I get in my car to go somewhere. If the family is along, it may be a spoken prayer. If I am alone, it's a silent prayer. I pray that I will harm no living thing as I pass by, that the Lord will protect me from being in or causing an accident, and that I will have a safe journey. Because I am often in a hurry to keep appointments or meet deadlines, part of my prayer sometimes is that the Lord will get me through.

Then came the tie-up and a new perspective on freeway prayers. Sitting there immobile, I realized it wasn't enough to pray just for myself, but that everybody on the road had to be prayed for, and concerned about. I'm at the mercy of an accident or mishap far up ahead that brings every car behind it to a grinding stop. I can't turn off on a side road and go my own way. There are no side roads. There's no place to go.

My car may be working perfectly, and that's fine. But let someone I don't know and probably can't see have a flat tire and the almost immediate result is as if it had been my flat tire. Anybody's accident ahead of me on that freeway becomes my accident, for it brings not only him but me to a helpless halt.

So the message was that a prayer only for myself wasn't big enough. God, if he wanted, could have worked a unilateral miracle and somehow whisked me over the stopped cars and on my way. But it hasn't been my experience that he generally operates that way. At least, not with me. I am not only my brother's keeper. I am also the kept brother—for good and ill. In a world that is week by week becoming more interrelated, there is little solitary safety. We are bound together. If I am to be secure, everyone on the road must be secure. I can't pray, "Lord, get me through!" I have to pray, "Lord, get us all through."

Then it occurred to me that my new discovery was really a pretty old truth. It was the way Jesus taught his disciples to pray. That exemplary prayer which we so often and so automatically pray (incidentally, the Lord's Prayer is for *praying*, not just *repeating*), doesn't say, "Deliver me from evil." It says, "Deliver *us* from evil." There are evils from which deliverance can come only for all, if for any. The entire Lord's Prayer, from its very first word on, is a prayer in the plural. Not "My Father," but "*Our* Father." Not "Give me, this day, my daily bread," but "Give *us*, this day, *our* daily bread."

In our kind of world there's less and less standing room for those who would pray self-centered prayers. What Christian worth the salt he is supposed to be, would wish, for that matter, to eat bread, ringed by a silent circle of the breadless?

The world is more tightly bound together than we realize. Driving along happily in our little self-contained and, we think, self-sufficient independence—tank full, motor tuned, tread deep—it's easy to think the world exists for us. But let the lights flash and the traffic halt and suddenly we know how dependent we are, the strongest upon the weakest

In an exasperated moment, one might be tempted to say that it is disgusting empirical evidence to support John Donne's truth, "No man is an island."

We are not moving alone down the highways of the world. We are affected by everything that happens to anyone on the way. Our security lies in their security. That is not simply a nice, shining platitude, but a pragmatic fact of life and faith. Being thankful that other cars on the freeway have good tires and that other travelers through life have adequate food and shelter is an exercise not only in sanctity but in survival.

Perhaps someday we shall learn how to discover our relationships before there is revolution or war, before there are riots or anarchy, whether at home or a world away.

For the traffic backs up so very quickly.

We're not home yet

The trip back home for Christmas started in Phnom Penh on December 19. Our chartered lumbering C-46 arrived in Singapore after an urgent, unscheduled and upsetting stop at Ho Chi Minh City (formerly Saigon), Vietnam, for engine repairs.

I went on to Thailand for a visit to the Kampuchean border refugee camps to say "Thank you" and "Merry Christmas" to our volunteer medical teams.

Then a flight to Hong Kong to connect with Pan Am 5 which would land me nonstop in San Francisco on Christmas Eve. Change planes. Catch a commuter flight to Burbank, the commercial airport nearest to my home.

From there it was less than half-an-hour's drive home. Youngest son, Mark, met me and drove. When we turned off the crowded freeway at our exit, I let out an audible sigh of relief. We were almost home. Only a little more than a mile to go. The tension began to drain away.

Then some inner message-center warned, "But we're not home yet!"

I half-remembered a statistic I had read somewhere. Something about the majority of travel accidents occurring within

what was it? A mile . . . a half-mile . . . of home? Maybe because the average driver is near home more often than he is
anywhere else. Or maybe because he figures too soon that he
is home free.

A car blundered unheedingly through a stop sign and Mark
had to slam on the brakes. My moment of premature relaxa-
tion was gone. Indeed, we weren't home yet!

It made me think of how ready we are to let down when we
get near "home." With the big part of the job over, all that
remains is the successful completion, the wrap-up—and it is
there we are accident-prone. More great projects, more exemplary lives, more prayerfully conceived actions have been
wrecked on the home stretch than this world dreams of. They
never quite made it because someone celebrated victory too
early, let down too soon.

We pay a great deal of attention to starters in the faith.
Starting is important. Nothing happens without starting. But
finishing is important, too, and I don't hear many sermons
about that. What if, at Gethsemane, Jesus had elected not to
"drink the cup"? After all, he had done most of what had to be
done. Why not ease up? If he had, then we would never have
had those portentous words from the cross: "It is *finished*."

Suppose Paul had decided not to go to Rome? He had, after
all, taken his share of long journeys for Jesus. But without
Rome could he have written, as he did to Timothy, "I have
finished my course"?

The highways of history are littered with the wreckage of
unfinished undertakings. They could have made a difference
for all time, but someone thought the trip was over. Then
misfortune. Close to home, but not home yet.

Back in the days of the Chatauqua circuit, a lecturer by the
name of Roscoe Gilmore Stott had a speech he called "Dying
on Third." In baseball terminology, he made the point that
the first batter up could hit .500, outrun anyone's throw to
first base, steal second, slide into third, but if that's as far as
he got, no run was scored. He could look very good, but if he

"died" on third, if he didn't make it home, it was as if he had never run at all.

When Paul wrote to the Ephesians, he had something to say about making it all the way. He said it involved putting on the whole armor of God, so that we would be able, "having done all, to stand." Not having done part of it. Not having gone half way. Not having made a decent beginning. But "having done all."

Sometimes we stand too soon.

The beginning is usually dramatic. Getting started is exciting. Creativity, compassion, adventure get the adrenaline flowing. Then, somewhere along the line, sameness sets in. The excitement of the new turns into the boredom of repetition.

Life begins to feel everyday-ish.

Ho hum.

We Americans are said to have a short crisis attention span. We want to deal with the boat people or the earthquake victims quickly and move on to something else. But it is not enough to initiate a relief effort, come up with great ideas, get something started. It quickly becomes a question of who will stay by for the long haul. Whose faithfulness, commitment and gentleness are deep enough to keep them going when the newness has worn off, when the task seems endless and the excitement has degenerated into hard, slogging work?

Some of the lines of a hymn have stayed with me from childhood:

I weary of the journey set before me,
Grow footsore 'ere I reach the mountain crest.

I know the feeling and I expect you know it, too. But then comes the rest of that unforgettable stanza:

But, lo! I hear a soft voice gently calling,
Come unto Me and I will give you rest.

Rest comes at the end of the journey.

When we reach home.

And we're not home yet!

Putting God on hold

The other day when I telephoned an airline office, a recorded voice announced, "All our agents are busy. As soon as one is free, your call will be handled." Then recorded music came on—bland, neutral music to fill the void and provide some semblance of life at the other end. In the days before someone thought of the music there was simply a click followed by dead silence, while I waited, impatience rising with each passing minute. The music was better than that, but not much better.

No one likes to be put on hold, although for heavy traffic telephone lines, it is probably as good a way as any of insuring priority.

But some priorities are inherent. For example, I cannot imagine that if we received a call from the White House it would be put on hold. Yet it happens all the time to the calls we get from God. The hold button at our end of that line has been worked to a nub. I suspect that his patience wears as thin as ours.

I once read an item in the English-language European paper, *The Herald-Tribune*. It was reported that J. Northcote Parkinson (of the famed Parkinson's Laws) had just formulated a new law. It was this: "Delay is the deadliest form of denial." In evangelical circles we hear a great deal about the sin of disobedience. We need to carry that one step further and acknowledge the sin of procrastination:

I will go, when—

I will give, after—

I will obey, but first—

One can always find reasons for delay, and sometimes they may even seem to be valid reasons. A close friend of mine and I were called to preach around the same time, and we went to university together. I was out mutilating homiletics in rural Oklahoma churches during those four years of study, but my friend insisted he wouldn't preach his first sermon until he had received his Ph.D. That was over thirty years ago. I am still mutilating homiletics, but my friend isn't preaching at all. He never did. Preparation is important, but *doing* is an important part of preparation.

Church buildings have been erected—and the practice is still common—by pastors and members who say that once the building is finished and paid for they will turn it into a great missionary base. That is like a doctor saying, "I will do my healing after the hospital is completed." Healing is what being a doctor is all about. It is not, "Let us do nothing now in order that we may do much eventually," but "Let us be faithful to our responsibility now and see what else God will entrust to us."

Are we ever fully ready for whatever the task happens to be? Is the author ever satisfied that his book has said it just right? Is the researcher ever finished with his research? There is always something undone, unsaid. There is always the elusive unknown, the risk of commitment, the taut moment before the sea parts. That is what faith is all about.

The story is told that at a summit meeting during World War II, President Roosevelt and Prime Minister Churchill were pressing Marshal Stalin to agree to a certain strategy. Stalin gave a reason for refusing. "Aha!" said Roosevelt.

"That is not the reason you gave the last time."

To which Stalin replied, "When you don't want to do something, one reason is as good as another."

Jesus had his own story for it.

A certain man had prepared a great supper and sent out invitations. The excuses were as immediate and lame as our own. One invited guest said he had bought a piece of ground and needed to go see it. (Had he bought it sight unseen?) Another had purchased five yoke of oxen and wanted to find out how they performed. (What kind of pig-in-a-poke purchase was that?) Another had just married and didn't want to take time out from his honeymoon (even for a free wedding dinner)!

The excuses sound like those of an anxious cluster of otherwise patriotic American citizens called for jury duty! The point of Jesus' story was that when we put God on hold while we do what we think is more needful, he may not be there when we finally get back to him. He just may have hung up and called somebody else, which is exactly what the supper host did.

"Later" is one of our most used words. In Spanish, it is the concept of *"mañana"*—tomorrow, any tomorrow, but certainly not today. Then I will see what I can do.

In the Old Testament we hear much about offerings of firstfruits. God's portion came right off the top. Nowadays we are more likely to be known by and for our lastfruits. Today's churches may be hesitant to talk about firstfruits, but Uncle Sam is not. He is very tough about his claim upon firstfruits, which he calls the "withholding tax." He's pretty sure that's the only way he will ever get what he requires.

God, too, I think.

Near the hold button on the hotline to heaven, these classic words would be appropriate:

If not I, who?

If not here, where?

If not now, when?

God's way with weeds

In my mother's vegetable garden I learned that weed-pulling, though not one of the world's more noble or prestigious jobs, is still a necessary one. Since the best garden, if left untended, soon becomes a ragged weed patch, I was called frequently from the pleasant pastimes of childhood to rid the garden of those "undesired, uncultivated plants growing in profusion so as to crowd out a desired crop."

(Those are Webster's words; I invented far more colorful ones to describe those scraggly spoilers of innocent springtime fun!)

I never forgave Adam and Eve, whom I blamed directly for all those thorns and thistles, crabgrass and cockleburs. Their presence in our garden was all part of the curse, as far as I was concerned. Come to think of it, I believe the garden is where I developed my antipathy for snakes, too, seeing them all as part of the punishment for original sin for which I took no personal blame.

But I knew I was stuck with the consequences.

With that boyhood background, I never had any trouble understanding Jesus' story about the wheat and the tares. I knew about wheat and I knew about weeds and—with some margin for youthful error—I knew the difference between the two. I understood the anxious desire of the farmhands to get the weeds out of the wheat field as soon as they had been discovered.

The parable is told in Matthew 13. A farmer who had sowed good seed in his field was told by his hired hands that poisonous weeds (a type of vetch, apparently, called "tares" in the King James' Version and more accurately termed "darnel" in the New English Bible) were growing among the wheat. The owner knew the strange seed had not been dropped by birds for it was too numerous. And he knew it was not a prank for darnel is more than just a nuisance—it is deadly. If the weed, which looks very much like wheat, is harvested and eaten with the grain, it will cause nausea, vertigo and possible death.

Sowing darnel in a field for revenge was considered a crime under Roman law. That is why in the story the owner said immediately, "An enemy has done it!"

Since parables are stories about life, Jesus later told his disciples that the good seed represented the children of the kingdom while the darnel was "the children of the wicked one." The parable depicted the conflict of the ages—right vs. wrong.

The laborers wanted to go immediately and pull up the poisonous plants, but the farmer forbade them to touch the darnel, saying, "Let both grow together until the harvest." It was a strange command, made even more strange by the devilishness of today's manifestations of evil.

Jesus is saying that good and evil should be allowed to grow together until his time—"the harvest."

If you have the uneasy feeling that evil is getting worse, you are right. Paradoxically, good is also getting better. Whatever else Jesus was saying in the parable, he certainly made it clear that there is a growth dynamic in both sin and righteousness. Neither can remain static.

Some who wring their hands over the proliferation and

satanic influence of sin today misunderstand its true character. It is in the very nature of weeds to grow.

I am troubled by some of my well-meaning friends who feel called by God to a ministry of pulling up darnel. They look around and identify an evil—it may be real or created in their own imaginations—and make its eradication their full-time Christian vocation. Not infrequently—in fact, most often—they found organizations to get others to help them. Both recruits and money for darnel-pulling activities are fairly plentiful, for it seems reasonable that we do God a service by getting rid of evil.

Yet no matter how well motivated the ministry or how dedicated the workers, Jesus specifically forbids trying to eradicate the darnel. His words are unequivocal: "Let both grow until harvest . . . ." And he didn't say that because he has any fondness for weeds.

Jesus has good reasons.

First, it is not easy to distinguish between wheat and darnel until both are fully grown. A spiritual amateur (and who isn't?) is sure to make mistakes. How tragic it would be if some tender wheat were plucked up by a zealous gardener with more enthusiasm than knowledge. Jesus would rather have the darnel grow than have a stalk of precious wheat destroyed. Most darnel-pullers I know don't have that same sense of values. If the faith of some be fatally injured in the process of fighting evil, it is easily passed off with the excuse that the results justify a few casualties.

Second, even if we could always tell the difference, our clumsy efforts to get at the darnel is apt to unintentionally uproot some of the wheat. Rather than allowing us to disturb those fragile roots, Jesus says he has reserved the separation for the surgical skill of his angelic harvesters.

Third, God has his own plans for the disposition of both wheat and darnel at the time of harvest. The wheat will be preserved in the Father's barn. The darnel will be sorted and burned. The burning is no task for spiritual children who just happen to have a box of matches.

Fourth, a preoccupation with darnel would leave us no time for involvement with the more constructive activities of kingdom gardening—tasks like sowing, watering, harvesting. The more darnel we pull up, the more seed the devil will sow. And he has an inexhaustible supply of infinite varieties. If you play that game with the enemy, he will guarantee you a full-time occupation.

Does this mean we are to show no concern for the deadly spread of evil through society? By no means. That which can be positively identified as darnel should be solemnly warned against. Things about which there is some uncertainty should be pointed out to the careless with prayer and humility.

But keep your hands off it!

Sowing, cultivating, watering and reaping in the wheat fields are much more satisfying activities than pulling up darnel.

And if Jesus be believed, safer, too.

Asking for trouble

Nobody in his right mind, we say, goes around asking for trouble. Along with the pursuit of happiness, the nonpursuit of trouble is held to be one of our inalienable rights. We've even given noninvolvement a quasi-legitimacy by affirming it in maxims and proverbs: "Let well enough alone," "No news is good news," "Ignorance is bliss" and "What you don't know won't hurt you."

They sound so authoritative and indisputable, don't they? Added together, they say, "Don't go around asking for trouble." It's a kind of mind-your-own-business, I'll-take-care-of-me-and-mine syndrome.

True, if a troubling need suddenly confronts us and looks us in the eye, we usually do something about it, with whatever degree of resignation. But as a life style—even a Christian life style—we tend to insulate ourselves against any involvement that impinges on our comfort, our conscience, our convenience.

I used to think that the priest and the Levite who saw the beaten man on that road which "went down from Jerusalem to Jericho" crossed over the road to the safe side. But now I'm not so sure. The story says only that they "passed by on the other side."

Maybe they were already on the other side. Could their sin have been not that they walked away from trouble, but that they didn't walk toward it? Perhaps they said, with self-justification, "Why go asking for trouble? Let well enough alone. What I don't know won't hurt me."

If that sounds disturbingly familiar, it could be because that is how we, too, rationalize our noninvolvement. But that is not what the Good Samaritan did. He went asking for trouble.

So did Jesus. Peter says of him, "He went about doing good" (Acts 10:38 NEB). That had always seemed to me to be a pleasant, certainly true, but not particularly dynamic text— until I realized the shattering implications for all Christians. For not only did Jesus *do* good, but he *went about* doing good.

In other words, Jesus went looking for trouble.

He sought out troubled people—those who were hurting, those who carried crushing burdens, those who knew the numbing experience of grief, those who were hungry, those who were sick, those who were dispossessed.

He didn't wait for trouble to come to him. He invited it. "Come unto me all ye that labor and are heavy laden," is the way he put the invitation. Not "Come unto me, all ye who have no problems, no worries, no cares." Not "Come all ye who are sanitized, deodorized, clean, well-fed, socially adjusted." Not "Come, ye who are self-supporting, financially solvent and trouble-free." Jesus asked for life's problem people. He asked for trouble. If we take him seriously that is what we do, too.

When our organization first projected the idea of *Seasweep*, a ship equipped to pick up or aid Vietnamese boat refugees in peril on the South China Sea, one government representative after another advised me, "Don't do it. You'll be asking for trouble." They feared it might be a monkey wrench in the wheels of international bureaucracy. In fact, it proved to be just that because as a result of media exposure, governments were forced to intervene in this shameful episode in human history. But I found out that governments, even more than individuals, dislike anything which disrupts the status quo. Following the example of the Master, we felt compelled to "ask for trouble." And to go out with *Seasweep* looking for it until we found it. Find it we did, and that story has been told. Hundreds of men, women and children are alive at this moment, many of them already resettled in lands of new beginnings, because a smitten conscience wouldn't allow us to listen to the professional advice of comfortable people.

If ignorance is bliss, pray tell me for whom? Not for those caught in the middle of tragedy, whether across the street or across the world. Not for those dying and helplessly watching the dying. Not for the children whose bellies are bloated and arms shrunken by malnutrition. Not for those trying to scratch out a crop from hard soil. There's precious little bliss at that end of the line, I can testify; and the more willful ignorance there is at our end, the less bliss at theirs.

There's something else that needs to be said, too. If those of us capable of changing the world do not go looking for trouble, sooner or later trouble will come looking for us. When it does, it often comes with gun in hand.

Though spawning their own inequities and suffering, revolutions and violence are usually caused by festering infections that were not lanced, sudden volcanic release of grievances that were never heeded, pent-up pressure of injustices never redressed. We failed to go looking for trouble, satisfied instead to live the safe, comfortable life in our evangelical cloisters. So trouble came looking for us—from Africa, from Latin America, from the Middle East. Make your own list.

We didn't do enough "going about." What we chose not to know did hurt us and is hurting us and will hurt us. No news may be bad news.

And as for letting well enough alone, where on this wracked and shaken planet can we find anyone well enough? The church was not commissioned to preserve the status quo, but to challenge it and change it. And when the church speaks with a prophetic voice and does prophetic deeds, it can expect the denunciation that comes to prophets. King Ahab assured Elijah he was "the worst troublemaker in Israel!" (1 Kings 18:17, TEV).

Go ahead and look for trouble.

Then do something about it.

Who does the hoeing?

Growing up as a barefoot farmboy in Mississippi, I learned more life lessons outside our little two-room school than I did inside. This is no reflection on my teachers. It's just that dirt-level observation and experience are tough competition for a classroom of theory.

For example.

Early on I learned that it is a lot more fun to harvest than to hoe. Or, for that matter, to plant. Few rewards can compare with that of plucking the bounty of the earth which represents the fruit of your labor. Harvesting is dramatic, fulfilling. You see what you get and you get what you see. In the earlier stages, there is nothing—or, at least, very little—to see. In fact, when you plant, you cover up even what you started with.

It always seemed to me the hoeing started the day after planting, although I know now that was a childhood illusion arising out of my joyless anticipation while we waited for the seed to sprout. But when the hoeing did come, I thought it would never end. Trying to clear away crabgrass from tender cotton plants in muddy bottomland under a blazing Mississippi sun when the humidity is a stifling 80 percent is about as accurate a description of hard work as you are likely to find.

Not that harvesting isn't hard work, too; but it's different. That's the payoff. The sense of reward represented by autumn's harvest can cause you to forget the less satisfying work of spring and summer.

But not even that can compare with luxuriating on mounds of sweet-smelling hay piled safely in the barn or playing among the golden ears of corn, shucked and banked high in the crib for winter's need.

Ah, bliss!

Of course, it goes without saying that there would be no autumn harvest if there was no drudgery of spring and summer. Full barns require soil preparation, planting and hoeing. The "winning run" in baseball may top off all the prior runs, but the first was as necessary as the final one, even if the crowds didn't leap to their feet and tear the stadium apart early in the game.

Yet in our world we overemphasize finishing, underplay starting. The guy who pitched the first eight innings goes to the dressing room unheralded, while the man who retired the last batter rides on the shoulders of his teammates. But without the starters who endure the dirty job, the unrewarding assignment, the unsung early things, there could be no finishers, reapers, winners.

It is as true on the mission field as elsewhere.

And the sad fact is that most mission societies today have shifted their emphasis from planting and hoeing to harvesting and storing. Most missionary energies and resources go toward places where seed has already been sown. They fertilize the soil to keep the yield respectable; they protect what is already in the barn.

What my father used to call "new ground"—characterized by stumps, roots and stones—gets little attention.

Look at the facts, courtesy of Dr. Ralph Winter, director of the U.S. Center for World Mission:

Fact 1. This is a world of four billion-plus people.

Fact 2. One billion of these people are Christians.

Fact 3. One billion non-Christians live among Christians, reachable by expansion of the church within its own culture.

Fact 4. The rest—some 2.4 billion—live outside of direct contact with indigenous Christians. They are reachable only by cross-cultural evangelism.

Now here comes the shocker. In spite of these facts, 91 percent of the missionary force—to say nothing of the number of indigenous Christians themselves—is assigned to maintain and strengthen the established churches, while only 9 percent is sent to work in the tough new ground of cross-cultural evangelism.

Which ought to give rise to some hard questions. Are our priorities topsy-turvy? Can we ever evangelize the world with such a strategy? Are we more concerned with success and results than with tough pioneering?

An example: Reaching traditional African religions (a phrase to be preferred over "animists") was easy during the colonial era and so large numbers of missionaries were assigned to this harvest field. Reaching Muslims was—and is— tough, so not many people have been engaged in watering and cultivating this field where the harvest is sparse.

Since most missions took with them no plans to leave the places they entered (which means, in essence, they didn't plan for success), they now find it hard to withdraw personnel. Not to say they aren't trying. Take the so-called "faith missions" (a term, incidentally, with which I have problems because *all* missions are faith enterprises, not just those independent ones with no denominational backing). Anyhow, the faith missions, which formerly criticized the idea of fraternal workers sent from a church body at home to another one overseas, are now trying to educate their constituencies to the new revelation that "nationals can do the job better than we can."

It is not coincidental that this new revelation just happens to parallel two other trends: (1) Decline of funding for missionary support and (2) difficulty of obtaining visas for missionaries.

I know the Lord told us to pray for workers to be thrust into the harvest, but I don't think he'd mind if we broadened our praying to include petitions for some who will cultivate, plant and hoe among the 2.4 billion.

He who is the Lord of the joyful harvest is also Lord of the footslogging and the hoeing.

Faithfulness and the present tense

In this country's so-called morality movement, I find a disturbing degree of ambiguity and not a few contradictions. For one thing, I observe that it selects moral issues on a highly individualistic and subjective basis.

Issues picked for a demonstration of moral outrage do not cover the full biblical spectrum. Rather, they seem to reflect a preoccupation with middle-class values oriented to our more limited Western mindset.

Examples: Pornography is bad, but the obscenity of nuclear war comes in for not a mumbling word. The absence of prayer in the public schools is an evidence of a degenerate society, but the lack of justice in the world is not a Christian concern. Abortion is sin (even murder), but the death of thousands of infants from malnutrition is merely unfortunate.

In other words, evangelicals can be remarkably sanguine about issues which seriously affect the rest of the world but do not directly touch us.

Consider this excerpt from a letter I received from a clergyman who is a leader in the battle against what he calls "secular humanism." He wrote: "I think it is well established among Bible-believing Christians that children are eternally secure until the age of accountability (whatever age at which conscience strikes). If this is true, and if our humanitarian concern for man motivates us to raise money to feed the starving children of the impoverished countries of the world so that they can grow up and cross the age of accountability and then die and go to hell, have we really helped them?"

The letter writer was, according to his own testimony, completely serious. He was asking: Is it better to keep a hungry child alive so that he may grow up possibly to reject Christ and be doomed, or to let him die in childhood and be assured of salvation?

Let's not even stop to wonder whether the writer would raise the same question if these were American children. Especially if they were his own children. But let's do ask one question: Where is it guaranteed that all well-fed children growing up in so-called Christian countries will accept Jesus Christ?

Without getting into a theological analysis of assumptions and implications inherent in the question, let's do some supposing.

First, we will have to suppose there is some validity to the man's question. Leap that gap with me, if you can, difficult as it is, so we may go on.

Suppose some of those fed and healed do later on accept the Savior. Should all be allowed to die simply because we cannot determine which ones to feed? Jesus instructed his disciples, "Let the little ones come to me" (Luke 18:16 NEB). It is not a restrictive invitation. Jesus set no limitations, imposed no tests of future orthodoxy, called for no ideological triage.

Suppose one of those starving children could have become a great evangelist to his people and suppose tens of thousands might have been converted through his ministry—but we decided not to take the risk and feed him. Now suppose it's not tens of thousands, but only hundreds converted. Or tens. Or one. Or none. At what point does the investment "pay off"? And who does the measuring?

I think of the human genealogy of Jesus—those "begats" in Matthew 1. Some of those links, it seems to me, did little more than keep the chain intact. But that was enough. In what chains of eternal destiny may some of today's children prove to be a link? For that matter, what and who were the imponderables in the chains that gave us our own life and ministries?

Of course, many of these unfed children will not simply die; they will experience a long, living death because of mental retardation due to malnutrition. By withholding food from a child, you have not "killed it and thereby assured it of heaven" (I know it sounds terribly crude, but that's what the letter implied). Rather, you may have created for that child a living hell of mental and physical deficiency.

But enough of abstractions.

I find it hard to be philosophical or theoretical or hypothetical when, in a refugee camp on the edge of Kampuchea, I stand in front of a swollen little eight-year-old girl who is suffering from *kwashiorkor*.

She is gasping for breath. The doctor tells me it takes all her strength simply to breathe. Her protein level is so low that her body is now feeding on her blood. I see the anguish in her mother's face. The doctor tells me the child can be saved. Just a little extra food and some simple vitamins.

Suppose you were standing there. What would you do? That's what I asked my letter-writer, but I haven't received an answer.

I know what I did not do. I did not get into a debate with myself over theological implications of feeding her. Instead I responded immediately out of Christian compassion—not simply humanitarian concern—and told the doctor we would pay for the nutritional program that keeps not only that girl, but hundreds of other children, alive!

Suppose you had been that child's mother, standing by? What would have constituted the more effective and convincing Christian witness to you? Hearing "I'm really doing your child a favor by letting her die"? Or hearing "I will do my best to give your child life"?

To ask is to answer.

I believe there is plenty of scriptural motivation for doing good. I also believe something is very wrong with a Christian who must wait for chapter and verse validation before responding to human need. At times we may need the prodding of Scripture to overcome our reluctance to do good; but we should never need assurance that doing good is permissible. Some actions are self-validating. It's not a matter of not knowing what God wants us to do, but of knowing only too well.

Faithfulness operates in the present tense. The future belongs to God. He does not expect me to do his work. He does, I think, expect me to do mine.

Sword without a handle

Except for one piece of equipment, all the materiel stock-piled in God's armory and awaiting our requisition is defensive in nature. Belt, breastplate, foot covering, shield, helmet are all designed to offer protection from attacks of the enemy.

The one exception: ". . .the sword of the Spirit, which is the word of God" (Eph. 6:17). A sword is for offensive action. For laying to.

It is not always cowardly to employ defensive tactics when you are being assailed by fiery darts. There are times when it is more prudent to hunker down under the Christian's armor and wait out the attack. That's the heroism of hanging in there, and it has been my experience more than once.

But there are times when it is necessary to go on the offensive, to unscabbard the double-edged sword. When that time comes, certain facts about swords ought to be remembered.

In some situations, a sword can look attractive indeed. When you've absorbed blow after unreturned blow, taken it on the chin or wherever, been patient, long-suffering, sweet and kind as a Christian ought to be, the thought of un-sheathing the sword and letting somebody have it right be-tween the spiritual ribs can be terribly appealing. I know.

Furthermore, it doesn't appear to be very dangerous, especially when you can lunge out from a well-padded position inside all that protective armor.

In fact, going after some gross sinner or some exasperating saint can be enormously satisfying to the flesh. It is frequently done with gusto, made easier because the wounds inflicted are emotional and spiritual instead of physical. The lacerations are on the heart, not on the body. Tears flow instead of blood. Discouragement, not death, results.

So we sometimes use the Word of God and the words of God as swords, fearlessly and gleefully. The choice of blade and the style of handling may vary, but most of us are clearly out for blood. Some employ the broadsword approach that requires both hands. Lifted high, it is brought down with a mighty blow that cleaves asunder, splits, dismembers—publicly, indiscriminately. At the other end of the scale is the stiletto style, front or back, requiring closer, more private, almost surreptitious contact, but no less deadly. In between is a whole range of swords and recognizable techniques of spiritual swordsmanship.

So a word of caution seems to be in order. Those who delight in aggressive Christian swordplay need to remember that the sword of the Spirit has a critical difference from other swords. Your usual, everyday sword has at least three distinct parts to it: blade, guard, and handle or hilt. The blade has a cutting edge along its length and may be two-edged. The handle provides a safe, smooth grip. The guard prevents your hand from sliding accidentally down onto the cutting edge when you're thrusting the blade into someone's vitals.

A friend of mine once pointed out to me that the sword of the Spirit has only one part: blade. All blade. No exempt handhold for the wielder. Who picks up this sword to use as a weapon is as subject to its judgment, its sharp discernment, as the one to whom it is pointed. So swordsman, beware! You can't use it on others without at the same time using it on yourself.

This single offensive weapon in the Christian's inventory needs to be handled carefully, gently, even gingerly. Unless your hands are covered with tough, unfeeling calluses, grasping the sword barehanded will mean blood on your own fingers—your own motives weighed, your own actions judged. And anyone who has become calloused in the use of the Word of God is in a dangerous spiritual condition.

Nothing about the sword of the Spirit allows me the reckless impunity of the handle while it gives you the hazard of the blade, or vice versa. "God will judge you in the same way you judge others," the Bible says, "and he will apply to you the same rules you apply to others" (Matt. 7:2 TEV).

That ought to make us a little slower to reach for the sword, a little more meticulous in its use. "For the word of God is living and active, sharper than any two-edged sword, piercing to the division of soul and spirit, of joints and marrow, and discerning the thoughts and intentions of the heart" (Heb. 4:12). *My* heart, too. *My* joints and marrow. *My* soul and spirit.

Don't try to craft a handle for this sword and tape it in place. I have—and can show you the scars as proof that it doesn't work. God is no respecter of persons, or of fingers. He offers no favored-person or favored-nation status. He doesn't say, "This commandment, this precept, this stewardship applies to those other people, but not to you." He doesn't say, "You were meant to be at the head of the line." There are no "firsts in the kingdom" when it comes to hearing and obeying the Word of God.

Sword of the Spirit.

Sword without a handle.

Use it with care and gentleness.

It cuts both ways.

What happens if the sound goes off?

There was giggling in the family room. Something had gone wrong with the television set—the picture was there but the sound was missing. It turned out on investigation that our canine family member, Tam O'Shanter, had clinked his name tag against his rabies vaccination tag and the sound was exactly the same pitch as the automatic sound button on the set.

My dog had rendered the actors mute.

They were still making earnest mouth movements, but nothing came out. It was funny because the characters in the sit-com were taking themselves so seriously without communicating anything.

I began wondering if Christians might look as ludicrous if our "sound" got turned off. Would our actions be enough to validate our testimony? Or to ask the question another way: If you were on trial for being a Christian, would there be enough evidence to convict you?

Or do we depend too much on words? Consider this: To prove our orthodoxy, we draft a statement of beliefs. We debate it, amend it, and finally adopt it. After which everyone goes home proud of having been on the firing line of faith. Now I'm not against statements of faith. I just wonder why it

is that usually we measure orthodoxy by what we say or sign
rather than by what we do?

For one thing, I guess, it is easier to say something than it is
to do something. For another, we are a word-oriented society.
Christians, especially, put a lot of emphasis upon passing resolutions and signing statements that are supposed to add
credibility to our ministry.

I get a fair share of opportunities to append my name to one
kind of statement or another. For the most part, I pass them
by—not because I necessarily disagree with the statement or
think resolutions are unimportant or that words have no
significance.

I'm just bothered that too many judgments are made solely
on the basis of whether a person has signed the right com-
bination of words or has endorsed a resolution that speaks to
"the pressing issue of the day." Words alone don't make a
Christian authentic any more than "In God We Trust" on a
coin makes it genuine. Counterfeit coins carry the same
words. Content, not words, determines authenticity.

Look at the reports coming out of church conventions. Almost without exception, the emphasis is upon what was
said—and, amazingly, we describe those exercises in ver-
bosity as "actions"! Recently I read such a story describing
the actions of a convention in terms of four resolutions that—
it's true, so help me—"denounced," "supported," "opposed"
and "deplored" various issues. And it all happened without
anyone so much as leaving his seat in the convention hall.

The "action" part of it, I suppose, was in saying aye or
raising the hand.

Talk is still cheap. And so much of faith has become a talk
show. If I seem to minimize the verbal expression of Christian
faith, it is only because I am weary of seeing word replace
deed. John said the Word was made flesh so that we might
behold the glory of the Father. We need the continuing incar-
nation for the same reason.

Some time ago I was in Africa with a couple of my evangelical brothers. I think it is not an injustice to say that they have a special passion for the symbolism of statements and resolutions. We were returning from a project that had to do with the social and spiritual development of one of Africa's most primitive people. I think they liked what they saw, but they wondered why we weren't making more statements about poverty, injustice, human dignity, and so on. They felt we were short on words.

I told them: "What you have seen *is* our 'statement' and you will see us making that same statement all over the world." I confess now that at the time it seemed like an inadequate answer, even though I knew it was the truth.

Only later did I recall that Jesus said essentially the same thing when John's disciples asked him if he was the real Messiah. Jesus didn't resort to a ringing declaration of divinity. He simply said: "Go and tell John what you have seen . . . the blind receive their sight, the lame walk, lepers are cleansed, the deaf hear, the dead are raised up, the poor have the good news preached to them."

What an utterly convincing statement! What more would mere words have added? Truth was authenticated by the deed. When that happens, even if the sound goes off, the witness will continue.

Stewardship of the ninety

For as long as I can remember, I have heard sermons about the offering of the tenth. Tithing, it is called. I practiced it even before I became a personal believer in Jesus simply because from my childhood, my mother taught me that was the right thing to do. The tenth belonged to God, she instilled in me.

Given as a part of Old Testament law, it is probably best known because of Malachi 3:10, that great passage about bringing the tithes into the storehouse. Jesus put his approval upon the practice (Matt. 23:23). Tithing is not only an efficient way of giving but a biblical way—ten percent off the top.

But I get the feeling that many of us think once the ten percent is out of the way, the rest is ours, scot-free, to do with as we please. In our concern to be biblical, we overlook the fact that stewardship has something to say not only about the top ten percent, but also about the other ninety.

And that is where we reveal what we think is important. It is in the ninety, not in the ten, that we publicly and conspicuously witness to what we really believe are the priorities and implications of discipleship.

Too often stewardship is promoted on the grounds of what it will do for the steward. Of the tithe, God indeed says, "Test me in this . . . and see if I will not throw open the floodgates of heaven and pour out so much blessing that you will not have room enough for it" (Mal. 3:10 NIV). But far from being a *quid pro quo* business transaction, is this not a call to those who already claim to be committed? Commitment comes first. As love can never give enough, so commitment can never give enough, never do enough. And total commitment, like true love, keeps no ledger. Love is its own reward. When our attention is focused upon what we hope to get, we are in no frame of mind to give what it takes.

Preaching which offers physical comfort, financial security, spiritual tranquillity as a payoff for following Christ is heresy. The more deeply we love, the more vulnerable we become. Only when we do not care, does it not hurt. Similarly with commitment, only when we do not care, does it not cost.

Unfortunately, we seem to have attached the payoff principle to all that we do and are and have as Christians. Because we are God's people, we think we deserve special privilege. There is indeed something special about our situation, but it is special responsibility, not special privilege. We are among the elect, but note to what we have been elected: Servanthood. Becoming a child of the King is a license for being a servant, not a franchise for demanding service.

Like our Lord, it is our role not to be ministered unto, but to minister. This is the reverse of everything that "important people" have ever believed or wanted to believe about themselves. It's not an easy proposition for Christians to accept. I know I have problems with putting it into practice. I want to go to the head of the checkout line and at times (dare I confess it?) I am tempted to take the parking space reserved for handicapped persons. Having gone this far, let me tell you the rest of it. I like to get my way, even if that means "being ministered unto" instead of ministering.

All this real-life wishing and living, all this authentic witnessing for good or ill, falls somewhere in the ninety percent. So does our house and the car in the garage. So does the use of a skill, whatever it is, however we use it. So do our financial investments, which are in some way affecting the world for better or worse. So does the amount we spend on an evening out, a dinner in, a suit of clothes or a gown.

One cannot set a Christian life style for others and I believe it is not Christian to try it. It takes no deep understanding to know that wealth is relative. Poverty in one part of the world is affluence in some other part. It is as easy to say of little as of much, "Lord, this is mine—hands off!" But where you are and where I am, our handling of the ninety as well as our handling of the other ten percent, in some clear way says something eloquent about our Christian commitment, perhaps more than we care to have said about it.

The widow's mite given at the temple appeared so great because what she had left was so little. I don't come off looking very good under that kind of measurement. In America, Christian giving for the most part is not terribly demanding. "Give until it hurts," the adage goes. But are we really giving at all if it doesn't hurt, if it doesn't cost us something? When David as king was offered free animals to be sacrificed to God, he established a worthwhile principle in the words of his refusal: "Neither will I offer . . . unto the Lord my God of that which doth cost me nothing" (2 Sam. 24:24 KJV).

But if we give until it hurts, then we must ask what does "hurt" mean? Is it anything more than a readjustment to a new commitment, the "expulsive power of a new affection"? Do commitments ever really "hurt"?

Perhaps stewardship is not so much giving up something as doing what one thinks is most important. Parents who modify their life style in order to give their child a college education do it not out of compulsion but out of joy. It's not your burden—it's your child!

I guess what I am thinking these days is that God is not so much trying to teach us fractions as to get us to understand that it all belongs to him—the nine dollars somewhere as well as the one dollar in the collection plate.

Maybe the question Jesus is asking each of us—and the one we had better be prepared to answer without embarrassment—is the one he asked about the thankless no-show lepers whom he had healed: "Where are the nine?"

It's about time

On my desk is an unusual clock, one of those electronic miniaturized marvels. Local time is normally displayed to the right of a small map of the world. But when I turn a knob, the time in any one of 24 zones around the world appears in its place and a tiny red indicator lights up to show where in the world it is. For example, at 9:00 a.m. on a Monday in Los Angeles, it is 7:00 p.m. in Cairo and midnight Tuesday on the South China Sea.

More than a useful gadget when international phone calls have to be made, it is a helpful reminder to me that my city, even the whole United States, is not the center of the universe. The day begins literally on the other side of the world, sweeps westward to us and then beyond. It is our day for a while, and then it is someone else's day. Each new day begins somewhere else and ends somewhere else, but it is ours, well, for a time. The clock on my desk says something to me about the timeliness of life everywhere.

The Bible makes frequent references to time. My concordance gives whole columns to passages in which the word *time* or its variations are used. One of the first that comes to mind is Ephesians 5:16, " . . . redeeming the time," which means—according to my own personal paraphrase—to use it wisely, making the most of every opportunity.

Not everyone in the world is as time-conscious as we are. Not everyone has a wristwatch, or even a calendar. Most tribal peoples cannot tell you how old they are or how many years ago something happened. I was with one tribe where any number over three simply became "many."

There is an unhurried flow of life in jungle villages, no signal bells or factory whistles to start or stop things, no schedules that demand obedience, no clocks to divide and subdivide the day. But the more conscious we or they become of the wholeness of earth and the hope of heaven, the more we appear to become aware of the significance of time. Clocks, though not catalogued as part of the whole armor of God, may be at least a useful piece of the Christian's supplementary equipment.

"Redeeming the time." The time that we do not exclusively own but which circles us, encompasses us, gives itself to us. More consequential than we have supposed is the crime of killing time, of wasting opportunity, of withholding caring, of assuming that the clock ticks only for us and that we have all the time in the world.

The new day, the new year, that wings westward brings with it all the burdens it has picked up along the way, and goes from us carrying our own fallout of good and ill. I turn the knob on my clock and the time appears for Phnom Penh, Cambodia. On this morning in California, it is midnight there. At this very moment, children are dying because governments waited too long either to help or to permit help. But *children* is too general a term, too impersonal, too generic. Children do not die. It is always *a child* who dies—a child loved by an agonized mother, a child of a father who is himself too weak to struggle for justice, too politically powerless if he did. Thousands of children die, but they die one by one, each an infinitely precious burden small enough for one mother's arms.

I turn the clock to Philippines time. At this moment, what is Dominga doing—she on Palawan Island whose young husband wanted her to drink the "bitter root" and thus induce an abortion because they could not care for another baby? There simply was not enough to share with another living soul, however tiny. I promised support and the baby was saved. That baby has come into the world by now. Boy or girl—I wonder which? One small, fragile new life finding a friendly place of warmth because we discovered, in time, what was happening in a neglected little corner of the world. So often, it is not that Christians do not care. It is just that they do not *know*.

I wonder about so many others around the world. Whatever the time zone, people are real flesh and blood, not merely statistics, and they are hurting. Everywhere, time is fleeting. How difficult it is to understand and accept the fact that time does not wait. It does not wait for legislatures to act, for governments to relent, for borders to open, for conditions to improve. It does not wait while we, insulated by distance, make up our minds, decide whether the need is great enough or dramatic enough or immediate enough or salable enough. The clock ticks on for those who have no clocks. The night, when no man can work, overtakes them as it overtakes us.

Time. It's the stuff of which life is made—theirs as well as ours. It's the stuff of which this year, this week, this very day, is composed. It is for redeeming.

How do we redeem it? The Living Bible puts those words from Ephesians 5:16 into a clear, sobering directive: "Make the most of every opportunity you have for doing good."

It may not be your last opportunity. But it could be someone else's.

Why fight the clock?

The hands of the apocalyptic clock stand at five minutes to midnight. In fact, that has been the time of night for as long as I can remember, and it would not be far wrong to say that it has been the time for 2000 years.

This is not to deny that we are closer to "end times" than ever before. We are—and events confirm it daily.

The *Bulletin of Atomic Scientists* has its own symbolic clock, predicting the nearness of nuclear doomsday. With the cold war intensifying appreciably, the minute hand on the scientists' clock has been moved from ten minutes before midnight to two minutes before—as close as it has ever been. Was atom-splitting the forbidden fruit that sooner or later will blast us from this only Eden we have left?

How is one supposed to act in the face of this inexorable tick of the clock toward the world's midnight? As apocalyptic problems multiply, I observe three attitudes.

Panic.

Paralysis.

Passivity.

Or you can choose a synonym for the last word. Indifference. Apathy. Anyhow, the syndrome expressed is it's-beyond-me-let-God-handle-it.

But sleepy nonchalance is not the best way to take it. Dramatic events of the end times are meant to stir us from our torpor and passivity. Isn't that one thing, at least, that Jesus means to tell us through the story of the five foolish virgins who let their lamps go out? Keep your lamp trimmed and burning, he said.

And as for the emotional paralytics who stand immobile before onrushing events much like a man watching in horror as a train in a railroad tunnel bears down on him, there is this to say: Being God's man or woman in times like these requires more than hoping for the best and waiting for the worst.

It means finding, somewhere between numb fear and dumb resignation, the spiritual adrenaline needed to do what we can do, and the faith that God will, in his own way and time, achieve his purpose. It means, in some sense, working *with* the clock, not against it. It means recognizing God's sovereignty over all events while accepting our personal responsibility to make use of those events.

But perhaps there is more panic than paralysis or passivity. For sure it is not a tranquil world. Events keep turning up the heat under our pressure cooker lives until we feel as if the lid is bound to blow. Economic difficulties are only one stress factor, but more than the other variables, it seems that interest rates and inflation affect us most keenly and most broadly.

A *Time* magazine (April 7, 1980) survey of psychologists and psychiatrists confirmed that "the pressures of inflation are sending many marginally stable patients over the brink." One psychotherapist said: "We're seeing a cumulative effect. When financial problems are added to internal problems, they tend to overwhelm people."

To say nothing of adding energy shortages, nuclear proliferation, international terrorism, political upheaval, unemployment and on and on, *ad infinitum*.

Said one psychologist: "People feel things are beyond their

control." Probably so. But one healing perspective might be to recognize that things, in fact, have never been in our control. Many heart attacks, strokes and stress-related breakdowns are undoubtedly brought on by our frantic attempts to control things which are beyond our control.

But the world is not out of God's control. Not now. Not ever. He is not a sleeping giant who bestirs himself only on special, potentially historic occasions. As the Amplified Bible puts John 5:17: "My father has worked until now. He has never ceased working. He is still working."

Midnight, as much as morning, belongs to God. God does not propose to abandon the world when the clock strikes twelve. He started the cosmic clock ticking, after all, and every event that has ever occurred came right on his prearranged schedule. The arrival of Jesus on the stage of human history was meticulously timed. In his letter to the Galatians, Paul climaxes a discussion of God's dealings with man in these words: "But when the right time finally came, God sent his own Son" (4:4 TEV).

But God is not only in control of *the* times. His activity is much more personal and intimate than that. In the psalms, David sings this comforting affirmation for all of us, *"My times are in thy hands."*

On Sundays we sing, "This is my Father's world," but on Mondays we act as if it belonged to whichever of the superpowers can first get its finger on the doomsday button.

It doesn't.

It belongs to its Creator.

And in the grinding tension between the nonchalance of doing nothing and the frenzy of trying to do everything, there is a point of dynamic balance that offers inner peace despite outer turmoil.

Working with God's clock will give you the serenity of being in harmony with the universe, not out of sync with it.

This is something like working with the law of gravity. Someone once explained to me that no one could build a plane that would fly until they learned they couldn't do it by disregarding natural forces. It took the inventors a long time to discover that it is the contour of the wing surfaces that provides "lift." They didn't discover that fact until they quit fighting natural laws and began using them.

Because the upper surface of a plane's wing is greater than the lower surface, the differential between pressures of the air passing over these top and bottom surfaces whisks a 630,000-pound airliner into the sky and keeps it there. That's simplifying it a bit, but it's the general idea. In any case, gravity is in the picture and it can't be turned off. Somewhere between being earthbound by gravity and nullifying it, there is a way to use it to fly.

So it is with apocalyptic events. While the clock ticks, God keeps on working. And it is helpful to remember that he works not only through Joseph, but through Joseph's brothers and even Potiphar's wife.

As with Joseph, all that God requires of us is faithfulness in the circumstances. At the end of our rope, we will find God waiting. He knows exactly when the rope will give out.

It is then we discover that not only we, but the rope, are his.

Where there's smoke . . .

It took the energy crisis to challenge that truism, "Where there's smoke, there's fire." Not that it isn't true still, but our new energy-consciousness causes us to remember that something else needs to be said.

I got to thinking about all this recently as I was flying over some trackless jungle. At least, it looked trackless from our altitude. When I saw a ribbon of smoke rising from that generous piece of nowhere, I thought, *Someone is down there.* Unless lightning was responsible, someone kindled that fire.

Much of the smoke in some parts of the world comes from the discredited "slash-and-burn" agriculture of primitive farmers who exhaust the soil in one place, move on and destroy more timber in order to have new planting ground. In other parts of the world, it spews out of the smokestacks of modern polluters. Some scientists believe this surplus of smoke from burning wood and fossil fuels is going to wreak climatic havoc as those tiny particles released into the atmosphere—along with volcanic ash—filter and reflect the sun's rays, producing a measurable cooling trend on the earth's surface.

The smoke signal I saw below from my airplane seat was a

reminder to me that in the ecology of man and God, the destinies of us all are bound together.

Maybe the old truism should be turned into a new axiom: "Where there's smoke, there's not enough fire." That is true also. Smoke is waste. What comes out as smoke should instead come out as energy. The more smoke, the less energy.

In California, people are generally more concerned with cooling than heating, but in those parts of our nation where even thermometers shiver in winter, homeowners have become very energy conscious. Wood-burning stoves have regained some of the popularity they had when I was a boy. It used to be that everyone could tell who got up early in the morning and who didn't, just by watching for the smoke from their chimneys.

But you can't read chimneys these days (except in Rome when the cardinals elect a new pope), because stoves now are more energy-efficient. The ads say they don't make smoke— they make heat. A smoking chimney is cause for alarm. It means that wood (at $100 or more a cord) is going up in smoke when it ought to be producing maximum energy.

I think it would be a good thing if we became energy-conscious in other aspects of life. For instance, I sometimes run into people who do their jobs with such sputtering, such egotistical display, such need for high visibility, that I wonder how much more might be accomplished if all that "smoke" went into the task itself.

Where there's smoke, there's not enough fire.

I was watching a television preacher the other night. His technique for getting audience response was so perfect that he paused at just the appropriate moments for the applause. When it failed to come once, he looked downright unsettled.

Making sure you get the credit uses up a lot of energy that could be going into the task. Lillian Dickson, a pioneer missionary who died recently in Taiwan liked to say, "You can do anything you want to do that needs doing, if you don't care who gets the credit for it."

In Scripture, men and women who waste energy in self-recognition receive absolutely no encouragement. Recall the story Jesus told of the Pharisee who came to the temple. Luke 18:11 says that he prayed "with himself." That's what happens when we grow overly concerned about how we look, how we sound, what impression we're making. The Pharisee's prayer was all smoke, no energy. Jesus then told of another man who also went into the temple to pray. He didn't try to impress anyone. He admitted that he was a sinner and asked for God's mercy. No smoke. Just basics. Jesus closed his story by asking which one really prayed.

The thirteenth chapter of 1 Corinthians contains a spiritual fuel supply with which we can stoke our personal furnaces every day. "Love is kind and envies no one," the New English Bible puts it. "Love is never boastful, nor conceited, nor rude; never selfish, not quick to take offence. Love keeps no score of wrongs."

No smoke. Pure energy.

We do not always, unfortunately, wish simply to love. We would rather have it noticed how loving we are. Not publicizing one's own acts of kindness or generosity is harder than keeping secret another person's sins. Most of us like to send up smoke signals which call attention to what we have done. And when the smoke spirals aloft, first a mere wisp, then a massive column that climbs high enough to mark our presence prominently, spiritual energy is depleted.

Thank God for those who do their jobs quietly and efficiently and dependably with a minimum of public attention, their interest in getting the job done, their loyalty to the Lord whose business it is they are doing. I stood on top of the giant Hoover Dam once, barely conscious of the soft whir beneath me as the powerful turbines generated millions of watts of valuable electricity. Afterwards, at a restaurant a few miles down the road, I was driven nearly to distraction by the flashing lights and ringing bells of two stupid pinball machines.

We Christians need to be more appreciative of the quiet ones, less awed by those who roar down Kingdom highways leaving a trail of smoke.

Sitting on the promises of God

I don't hear it much anymore, but when I was a boy, we sang with verve and gospel beat the song *Standing on the Promises*. After each stanza, the congregation swung into the chorus as if that was what they were waiting for. The harmony of blended voices of men, women and children gave richness as we finished off with that grand crescendo of faith, "I'm standing on the promises of God!" I'm not sure that I understood the implication of what I was singing, but its subliminal force lodged deep in my soul.

The words stir me now as I think of them, though these days we don't seem to be singing or talking much about the promises of God. Oh, we don't disbelieve them, but the prevalent pessimism is hardly compatible with eternal promises. When dark reality contradicts bright hope, the status quo usually wins out.

It seems there is more sitting than standing on the promises. The posture is a languid and listless one. No anticipation; no confidence. Little wonder, then, that we have become a generation of worriers. And most of the worry is not about real things, but about imagined and feared catastrophes, both personal and global. We go Jesus' admonition from the Sermon on the Mount one better, for we are anxious not only about the morrow (Matt. 6:34) but also about the moment—and the next millenium if time should last so long.

We inflict upon ourselves the demons of tomorrow's anxieties and then throw ourselves on the psychiatrist's couch to get them exorcised.

There is a fine line, I admit, between constructive concern, which God's people need, and destructive anxiety, which they do not. We were never promised a highway homeward without hurdles, hardships and hurts—only that, unfailingly, there would be Someone within reach. In a universe filled with black holes, uncountable galaxies, cosmic endlessness, that is no small comfort.

The tender shepherd psalm does make this unqualified statement: "I shall not want," but there is no promise that the path to pasture will avoid the barren place, the lonely wilderness, or the deep valley. Only that the Shepherd Lord will lead through every place the sheep is called to go. In the midst of some present personal tragedy, it is confidence in the Shepherd's leading which tempers my anxiety with patience. I am certain that where he is taking me will be a place different from the path over which I am walking now. After the turbulence of floods and the darkness of the valley of the shadow, there will be green pastures and still waters.

I know it.

Often I confuse *want* with *wants*. The translation in the Good News Bible helps straighten it out: "The Lord is my Shepherd; I have everything I need." Our expectation levels are easily lured from needs to wants. And some people will tell us there is no difference. If you want it, they assure us, God wants you to have it. These purveyors of an all-this-and-heaven-too theology are exploiting to a fare-thee-well the naive and childish materialistic attitudes which afflict so many. If God delivered everything these pious charlatans promise, earth would have more treasure than heaven.

Expecting more of God than we have any right to expect

can cause spiritual smugness if we get it, disillusion if we don't. But the other side of that is equally important. Not expecting of God what we should expect takes away the very means God has given us to cope with whatever comes. For sure, firmly standing on the promises provides power and lift. I like Victor Hugo's lines:

> Be like the bird
> That pausing in her flight
> Awhile on boughs too slight,
> Feels them give way
> Beneath her and yet sings,
> Knowing that she hath wings.

Where is your trust? In the slender boughs which bend and tremble under you, or in wings meant for soaring? Many of us act as if we're not sure we have wings, perhaps because we so seldom use them.

We may as well admit it. By ourselves, in our own strength, we simply can't cope. Life is too complicated, too overwhelming. The boughs upon which we think to rest securely prove too fragile. Savings. Investments. Relationships. Community. Nation. Which of them is substantial enough to carry our weight? Inflation erodes the savings of a lifetime. High interest rates make it difficult to buy—or sell—a home. There is lessening personal security; nowadays, thieves do more than break through and steal. They terrorize whole cities.

As a nation, we appear to be placing our trust increasingly in armaments, a bough that milleniums of world history have repeatedly demonstrated to be very insecure indeed. Family and personal relationships shatter. Children leave home or return home after their own breakups. Health deteriorates. Loved ones die. Things don't work out as we anticipated.

When the boughs break, if there are no wings, there is nothing.

Martin Luther, who knew something about standing on the promises, expressed it another way: "I have held many things in my hands, and I have lost them all; but whatever I have placed in God's hands, that I still possess "

Risky? Sure. Luther understood the risk when, before the ecclesiastical authorities, accused of heresy, he could say only: "Here I stand. I can do no other. So help me God."

That kind of affirmation comes from standing, not sitting, on the promises.

Have you checked out your posture lately?

Not everybody, but somebody

But I can't help everybody!"

When this hoariest of excuses for doing nothing is exhumed from mothballs, I usually quote Bob Pierce, World Vision's founder: "No, but you can help somebody!" Sometimes I follow that up with encouragement to start small and do something rather than sit immobilized by the magnitude of the task. I tell how important it is for each of us to take out a bucketful, and so on.

However, I am afraid that quick retorts may not evoke the desired response. I know they don't in me.

Besides, some of the people who say, "I can't help everybody!" are not alibiing but lamenting. They say it out of frustration and despair because they *are* helping someone, often many someones, and the undone task remains greater than the done. They seem never to gain on it. Far from being underwhelmed (as is, unfortunately, sometimes the case), they are overwhelmed, submerged, left gasping for breath in a great sea of need. No answer seems big enough.

Where does individual responsibility begin? And end?

I get considerable help on this when I look at the way Jesus ministered. He, too, lived in a sea of need. In that hot, dusty land of Palestine, blindness was common. Leprosy was a feared scourge. Sickness, hunger and sorrow abounded. Yet Jesus did not heal all the sick, feed all the hungry, raise all the dead. In his time and place, there were blind who never saw, lame who never leaped, bedridden who never walked, lepers who were never cleansed.

How many widows' sons were buried with no compassionate intervention? How many mothers-in-law never recovered from their fevers? How many wanderers in their wrong minds were never restored? How many epileptic or palsied children were never freed?

Surely Jesus knew he was only scratching the surface of need. How did he live with that knowledge? Theologians may provide additional perspectives, but a fact that I find personally instructive is this: In the Gospel accounts, *Jesus never turned away anyone who came within the scope of his awareness and ability to help.*

Of course, there was no limit to his power or ability, as there is to mine. But some had to fight for his attention— persisting their way through a cordon of protective disciples. Even when he thought to limit his ministry to "the house of Israel," a Canaanite woman, pleading on behalf of her daughter, breached his defenses. Insisting upon crumbs for her daughter, she received, instead, wholeness.

Scope of awareness. It was this which placed an inescapable compulsion upon him, and which places it upon us. When I see, when I hear, when I know, then something happens to me that has not happened before. It is then that the problem, the concern becomes mine.

When the knock comes to *my* door.

When the empty hand reaches toward *me*.

When the eyes look into *my* eyes.

Then I have to do something or surrender some piece of my Christian credibility. It is as simple as that.

And as complex as that. For the scope of our awareness is wider now than it was in the days of Jesus, wider even than it was ten years ago. There is still need in the world that we do not know about. But when a major tragedy strikes, we generally are informed by the time of the evening news. Nowadays, the small tragedy is more likely to be what we hear about last—the abandoned parent in a nursing home on the other side of town; the forgotten inmate of a prison just fifteen minutes away; the neighbor whose name we never took time to learn; the people we see every day who carry unsuspected crushing burdens.

Though needs had to come within the scope of Jesus' awareness in order to be met, I think the scope of his awareness was large and acute. Our scope, in spite of news coverage, tends to be limited, and our awareness not terribly sharp. We see and hear only the things to which we are tuned in. It is easier to catch a signal from Wall Street than from Main Street. From Washington than from Wewak.

The atmosphere around me is filled with signals, some of which are barely intelligible—the way the chattering radio sounds to me as I fly over a jungle in a small plane. The pilot knows what the radio is saying because his ears are attuned to the kind of information he needs.

Awareness, for us, is an ability that can be cultivated. We hear what we need to hear, what we want to hear, in the same way that a mother immediately catches the first cry of her awakening baby.

There are, sad to say, those who are afraid they *will* hear something, who avert their eyes lest they see something. How lonely to walk the streets of life, afraid to look up, afraid of what might be seen in even a fleeting glance at another face.

We avert not only our eyes but also our hearts, lest some compulsion leap across the gap and forever bind us together. For, even from our small experience, we know deep down that having seen, we cannot ever again unsee. Having heard, we will never again be able to unhear.

And unless conscience is dead, we will have to act.

"For God so loved the world that *he gave* . . . ." That is the penalty, and the incomparable reward, for being a follower of his Son.

Metric and other measurements

The other day on one of California's magnificent freeways I saw a new sign which indicated that my destination was still "67 miles (112 kilometers)" down the road. The parenthesis was what caught my eye. It reminded me that we are switching our ways of measuring things here in America to conform to the rest of the world.

We are going metric.

We'll measure our waist size in centimeters, not inches (can you get used to a Miss America whose dimensions are 86/63/91?), we'll buy our gasoline by the liter instead of the gallon, and we'll admonish ourselves that "A gram of prevention is worth half-a-kilogram of cure." On second thought, I doubt that we will. That last one just doesn't seem to make it.

I confess I haven't done very well at this kind of conversion, though many speedometers now helpfully carry dual sets of figures which translate miles into kilometers. But my real trouble comes with temperature conversions. Only with the greatest effort can I remember that 21 degrees Celsius means 70 degrees Fahrenheit and 50°C is not fit weather for man or beast.

However, metric is not the only system of measuring with

135

which we have problems. Consider success, for example. Usually we take the measure of a person's money and/or power. If a man or woman has a large income or wields influence, that person rates high on most success scales.

Most often we equate progress up the ladder of success with the accumulation of things. The more goods acquired, the more rungs climbed. Many of us can remember early days of marriage and the saving and planning which went into the first major purchase—a refrigerator or a bedroom suite or maybe a third-hand car. Each modest addition called for a celebration. We were getting somewhere. The rug on the once-bare floor proved it.

Nowadays, it seems that young marrieds want to start out with everything all at once, the way a motorist has to get up full speed on the entrance ramp so he can merge smoothly into the frenzied freeway traffic. I well understand their desire, but it makes me wonder what those who have always had everything will do if life becomes austere.

The apostle Paul knew "how to be abased, and how to abound" (Phil. 4:12). Maybe part of our national trouble is that for so many, the abounding must come first. I can almost hear Paul's wry inflection and see the twinkle of memory in his eyes as he nods his head and goes on to say: "I have been very thoroughly initiated into the human lot with all its ups and downs" (NEB).

It's neither the downs nor the ups that are the accurate measure of life, but Paul's preface: "I have learned, in whatever state I am, to be content." Some of us are not content even when for a time it's all ups. Perhaps we don't practice Paul's secret of coping: "I have strength for anything through him who gives me power." A part of that power is certainly the ability to convert the measurement. Not "How much do I have?" but "How well have I learned?"

I suggest the wastebasket test as another means of measure. What do you throw away? You can tell a great deal about a person by what he or she discards. What's in your wastebasket? Not just the normal debris of unused coupons, special offers and old magazines, but which traits, which attitudes, which habits? You say something about yourself—and to yourself—by what you throw away and what you keep. Obviously, you can't keep everything. In fact, to do so is a symptom of mental disorder. Wastebaskets are necessary. So is a discriminating judgment which tells us what to save, what to discard, and what to recycle. The measuring system on which we base those decisions may need to be converted to a different value base.

Another way of measuring is offered by my friend, Dr. Richard Halverson, chaplain of the United States Senate. He asks: What makes you mad?

It's easy—too easy—to get angry. Lord knows, I prove that distressingly often. The question is, what do you get angry at? That reveals volumes about a person.

So much of the time we get angry at the wrong things. A slight—real or imagined—can shatter marriages, destroy friendships, split churches. But we have a hard time getting mad at corrupt politicians or world leaders whose greed or mismanagement launches a wave of starving refugees. We keep our cool in the wrong places and in the wrong circumstances.

How can Christians think of the talent, hopes, aspirations and dreams locked behind the invisible walls of our inner cities and not get angry? How can we contemplate the increasingly easy—almost jovial—acceptance of possible nuclear destruction, without becoming mad? How can we see man's inhumanity to man anywhere and not feel our blood boil?

But when it comes to the small irritations—the dry-cleaned suit not ready on time, the waitress bringing eggs scrambled instead of over-easy, the Sunday morning Scripture lesson being read from the wrong version—these are things over which we can really build up a head of steam!

Don't we need a new measuring scale that tells us what is

worth a throbbing jugular? What if all that racing blood, all those bursts of energy, all that fearless denunciation were channeled into confrontations with the real things that are wrong with our world? Nothing could stand before that kind of holy anger.

When to get mad. And what to get mad at.

What to throw away. And what to keep.

How to measure success.

As the nation converts to metric, these also seem to be part of a new system of measuring that Christians need to learn.

Centimeter by centimeter, it's a cinch.

Punctuating life and death

Five days before his death in 1981, William Saroyan called the Associated Press to leave a statement: "Everybody has got to die, but I have always believed an exception would be made in my case. Now what?"

To at least some extent, I suspect, he was being facetious, putting words in his own mouth as he did with the characters about whom he wrote his short stories, novels and plays. Even so, there is more to it than meets the ear, not just for him but for all of us.

Mr. Saroyan was whimsical enough to say it out loud. Most of the rest of us, including us Bible-believers, have at some time had similar ponderments, though unvoiced and fleeting. The difference, it seems to me, is that, for the Christian, life can end with an exclamation point instead of a question mark.

This is not to say there are no question marks. Over the years I have heard many sermons preached on variations of "Now what?" Most of them charted everything from here to eternity with a precision that would do credit to the engineering of a spaceship. There was never any question in the speaker's mind that he had everything figured out from the last heartbeat on, down to estimated arrival time at various way stations, the latitude and longitude of heaven (and hell), and any and everything else. These "experts" did not, however, agree with each other. Protestants, who do not accept the Catholic concept of purgatory from which new arrivals have to prayed out or Limbo—a place bordering hell for the unbaptized—have a whole set of road maps of their own, each produced by someone who thought he had every twist and turn and crossing down pat.

I must confess that I am uneasy when I run into someone who thinks there are no question marks at all and who could, if asked (or even if not), draw a picture showing exactly what heaven is like. Personally, I don't care whether the streets are paved with gold. I am not even sure that streets are an indispensable part of it. Writers of inspired scriptural clues were faced with the immense problem of describing the indescribable, translating heavenly visions into sentences with subject and predicate. Sometimes, as in prayer, all that results are "groanings which cannot be uttered," or, as the Living Bible puts it, "such feelings that it cannot be expressed in words" (Rom. 8:26). I think there is nothing wrong with a few question marks. To assume that one has all the answers is to exhibit a sophomoric naiveté.

Where, then, does our confidence lie? What makes it possible for the Christian to come face to face with the realization that there may well be "no exception," and at the same time not be shattered by a "Now what?" The way, I think, is to recognize the adventure in what lies ahead. Not acceptance only, but excitement. Not needing to care so much about what, when one knows Whom.

On the cross, the Lord told the repentant thief, "This day thou shalt be with me in Paradise." It is the "with" that is important, not the where. Though Omar Khayyám had something a little different in mind in his Rubaiyat, there is an application here:

> *—and Thou*
> *Beside me singing in the Wilderness—*
> *Oh, Wilderness were Paradise enow!"*

I have always found confidence in the words of Jesus to his disciples: "And when I go and prepare a place for you, I will come again and will take you to myself; that where I am there you may be also" (John 14:3). Not many specifics. An earlier verse speaks of "many mansions" in the Father's house, but whether of marble or stucco or aluminum siding, I do not know. Or care.

We also don't know how we shall spend our time (talk about a "terrestrial" concept!) in heaven, what we shall look like, how we shall get around, how we shall relate to others including our loved ones, what we shall wear. Such things Jesus does not tell in nearly the detail that some of his present-day spokesmen presume to offer. On earth, he did tell his followers not to be concerned about what they should eat and drink and put on, and the advice would seem to be at least as applicable to heaven. What satisfies me is the assurance "that where I am there you may be also." If he is there, that's good enough for me. If I'm with him, what better place to be, even if I cannot begin to define "place" or have a floor plan in advance?

What, I wonder, is the value of trying to determine our "celestial" nature? I have been always a little baffled by a phrase in the Apostles' Creed: ". . . the resurrection of the body." I know what it means—that, somehow, personality and identity will be maintained. But a body as we know it? Here I am helped by the believer who freely admitted that he didn't know all the details: "It doth not yet appear what we shall be: but we know that, when he shall appear, we shall be like him; for we shall see him as he is" (1 John 3:2 KJV). Who needs Gray's *Anatomy?*

Well, you do it your way. This is my way to face the future

without getting so hung up on details that I have no energy or motivation left to do what God has given me to do in the present. If we—if I—can let God handle the question marks, the result will be a glorious freedom, a buoyant confidence, a release of enabling power.

Now what?

Now what!

As for me, I want to punctuate my life now—and my death when it comes—the second way.

If he asks for a scorpion

In the church service we had turned to the grand old hymn, *Spirit of God, Descend Upon My Heart*. As we sang it together, I could feel quietness and strength seeping into my bones. Then we came to a line that jolted me. I had sung it often, but had never really thought about it. "Teach me the patience of unanswered prayer."

Unanswered prayer?

What did the songwriter mean? What did I mean as I sang it?

You see, it is my conviction that no prayer prayed in the name of Jesus goes unanswered. It may not be answered as I think it should be or in the manner I carefully outline for God, but that doesn't mean it isn't answered.

Maybe the words were telling me that if I just hang in long enough, I can get my own way, self-destructive as it may turn out to be. They seem to suggest that if we are fervent enough, persistent enough, God will sooner or later throw up his hands and say, "Okay, you got it—and shut the door on your way out!"

Now there may be that kind of prayer, but, if so, it's not the kind of praying I want to do or the kind of answer I want to receive.

I am wary of that approach because of what I pray in the Lord's Prayer. We start with "Our Father . . ." Why is it, then, that having freely approached God as Father, we suppose he will not act like a father when we tell him what we want?

Many a father's heart is saddened at Christmas by having to refuse his child a gift on which the child's heart is set. It may be because the father is out of work and cannot afford the gift (certainly not a problem with God). Or maybe the money could be better used for other family needs. Or perhaps the child is still too young for the gift desired.

The father, being wiser than the child, less self-centered, knows what the child does not know. His refusal to say yes is a caring, not an uncaring act. Given the circumstances and the consequences, "No" or "Not yet" may be a more loving answer than "Yes." I know from my own experience as a parent that it is sometimes more painful to refuse a request than to grant it. It isn't giving in that most severely tests parenthood, but holding back.

A parent naturally wants the best for his child. How much more does God? Remember how Jesus illustrated the character of God: "What father among you, if his son asks for a fish, will instead of a fish give him a serpent; or if he asks for an egg, will give him a scorpion? If you then, who are evil, know how to give good gifts to your children, how much more shall your heavenly Father . . . ?" (Luke 11:11–13).

And would not the reverse also be true? What father, if his son asks for a serpent, will not give him a fish instead? Or if he asks for a scorpion, will not give him an egg? How much more will our heavenly Father?

Our impatience comes when we do not recognize what is for our ultimate good. God's version of a fish or an egg may look less attractive than our image of a serpent or a scorpion. Our vision is limited. Our judgment is flawed. Our wants tend to be selfish ones because we live in the "right now." If we get something that looks the way we suppose a good thing should look, we are satisfied and say, "Praise the Lord, my prayer is answered!"

Is God impressed by our fist-pounding and heel-kicking tantrums even when we try to dignify them by calling them prayers? Hardly. No parent would be impressed.

Perhaps that is why, in the Lord's Prayer, we don't get very far from "Our Father . . ." until we get to "Thy will be done." Prayer is not just a list of gimmes from a child sitting on the lap of a cosmic Santa Claus. It is communication with One who is wisdom and love. The cattle on a thousand hills are his, but I come to him in prayer not so much for a few head of cattle as to be reassured that *he* is there—and here—and that he cares about what happens to me. His hand is more important than what's in it. God is more than a heavenly piñata from which, if I pound hard enough, goodies will drop out.

There is another verse about prayer that I often have reason to recall: "Whatever you ask in my name, I will do it, that the Father may be glorified in the Son; if you ask anything in my name, I will do it" (John 14:13–14). I think we have paid more attention to the "anything" than to the "in my name." The latter does not just validate a request by being tacked on at the end, but represents a whole way of looking at life.

Can we honestly pray in Jesus' name and at the same time, like a spoiled child, insist on our own way? And does there not come a point in our praying when asking must stop and accepting begin?

Many of my prayers have not been answered as I thought they should have been. Thank God for that! Joseph, in the pit, must have prayed for deliverance. On the way into slavery, he may have sighed, "God did not answer. Lord, teach me the patience of unanswered prayer." But God, seeing down the dusty road to Egypt and beyond, was building an answer beyond all that Joseph could imagine.

Unanswered prayer?

I know now that I've never had a prayer God didn't answer. His way.

Let God put the squeeze on you

Some sociologists are calling this the evangelical era. Recently I've been thinking about some other terms. Like the decade of deluged disciples. Or the period of waterlogged witnesses. Or the season of sated saints.

For sure, no people in any place at any time have ever had more opportunities for growing in the faith than we have. Just look around you. Religious radio. Religious television networks. Bible study groups. Neighborhood prayer meetings. Spontaneous conversations in unlikely social situations about what my mother called "spiritual things." More religious books than ever. Conferences, retreats, congresses, festivals, rallies, seminars. All adding up to an unparalleled store of information available to believers.

But since so much is happening *to* us, why isn't more happening *because* of us? With all that input, where is the output? Agreeing that many things are being accomplished by the commitment of a few, I still have the uncomfortable feeling that a great deal more is going in than is coming out.

I observe an attitude which says that watching, listening, feeling, absorbing are our primary Christian responsibilities. We are terrific watchers and listeners. Nonparticipative forms of worship, in which ministers and choirs perform for us, have bred a generation of spectators. We are also big on feeling and absorbing, and even while we reject some of the more bizarre forms of group therapy, we have developed our own styles of spiritual navel-contemplation that make us more narcissistic with each passing fad.

No, I'm not minimizing the acquisition of information or the expansion of understanding as critical factors in Christian maturing. But knowledge is to be used, not hoarded. Hearers of the word who don't become doers, the Bible says, are like a man who sees his image in a mirror and then forgets what he looks like (James 1:22–24). If not acted on, the word fades away as a forgotten image.

With some reasonableness we pilgrims can argue that we have arrived at this point in our faith only with much struggle, and who is to say when we know enough, have enough, believe enough to return something to the reservoir? So we go back to the same seminars and lectures (repeaters even get a discount) year after year for more input.

In our zeal for spiritual self-improvement (nothing wrong with that, *per se*), we soak it all up, trying to hold every drop, absorbing until we're positively dripping, bloated, always taking without giving back. Being a "disciple"—a learner— was never intended to turn Christians into one-way sponges.

Still we pray, "Lord, fill me." I don't recall ever hearing, "Lord, empty me." The thought of being emptied is not a pleasant one, but emptying is what makes a sponge good for something. It's not bad to feel "all wrung out" if you know where to get filled up again.

Taking without giving back. We don't like it when people do it to us. "Sponging" is what we call it. Scripture has something to say about spiritual spongers. After wisely advising, "Each of you must be quick to listen," James soon adds, "Only be sure you act on the message and do not merely listen" (James 1:19, 22 NEB). In my copy, I have underlined *act*

When I was an undergraduate student after World War II, with my tuition being paid under the G.I. Bill, the danger of becoming a professional student ranked low on my scale of personal hazards. I have observed, however, that the longer you stay in the educational system, the harder it is to move from the halls of ivy to the alleyways of reality. Nonetheless, sooner or later, you've got to start turning something back into the system.

Granted, there's a certain attraction in studying theory, whether it's economics or theology. In religion, that's one way to keep faith at arm's length, celestial, undirtied. No sweat. No smells. Everything tidy. It's not until you begin giving out that you take on the crushing burden of caring.

I've never understood why history marks those who withdraw from the world as the supremely righteous people. There indeed have to be meditative components in all our lives. Mountaintop experiences, we call them, times when we sense the power and presence of the Spirit and feel renewed. But renewed for what? It's nice to hear a sermon on the mount, but that's not where we live. When Jesus came down from the mount, a leper was waiting for his sermon in the valley. When Jesus arrived at the bottom of the Mount of Transfiguration, an epileptic boy desperately needed to be touched by his glory and power.

John puts it straight: "It is the man who does right who is righteous" (1 John 3:7 NEB). In my copy, I have underlined *does*. Righteousness, he says, is not hearing right, not talking right, not seeing right. It is *doing* right.

The test is in the output.

Another thought. We're not in business to insure our own spiritual health any more than someone becomes a doctor to make sure he himself won't get sick. His knowledge of health and medicine may help him avoid a few things which the rest of us are ignorant about. But doctors have a passion to do something for other people, and sometimes—in the pace of the doing—they place themselves beyond their own healing.

That's a different attitude from soaking up everything for one's self. Did you ever wonder why sponges are packaged moist and damp? It's purely a marketing technique. Check it out the next time you're in a supermarket. You'll see that a full sponge looks much more appealing than one squeezed dry. But spiritual health just can't be gauged by the quantity of the input.

So go ahead and let God put the squeeze on you. Chances are you are robust enough to stand it—and anyhow, if you're squeezed dry in the process of caring and loving, he is the source of renewing. Jesus puts it correctly for our time and for all time: "Your care for others is the measure of your greatness" (Luke 9:48 LB).

In my copy, I have underlined *others*.

Baring one another's burdens

Forgive me, please, for altering the spelling, but that revised version seems to describe the standard of a lot of present-day practice. I know, of course, that the biblical admonition is "Bear one another's burdens, and so fulfill the law of Christ" (Gal. 6:2).

That's *bear*, not *bare*.

I don't hear a lot about bearing other people's burdens these days, or about the law of Christ, which is the law of love for that matter. Rather than obey, which is hard, we have distorted the command, which is easy.

If you are the one who should be sharing a burden, the distortion may be only a discourtesy. If you're the agonized bearer, however, the experience can be devastating. Have you discovered that fellow Christians often find it less demanding to gape and cluck than to love and trust?

Baring is definitely easier than bearing.

There is something in the human heart that revels in scandal. But Christians manage to cloak their carnal curiosity and voyeurism with an avowed righteous motivation ("How shameful are the sins I have not committed").

Next we want to dig into the whole story, find out who is

"guilty" of what, suggest a repair formula, get a quick prayer fix, so that all will be put back as it was. And if it isn't fixed within our self-arranged time schedule, we turn the person or persons over to the judgment of God and announce that we are no longer responsible. But a couple of things seem not to occur even to those who genuinely wish to be helpful.

First, "as it was" may not represent a new success but the old failure—not a healing, but a Band-Aid job on whatever caused the burden in the first place. Second, we tend to see burdens in terms of problems to be solved rather than in terms of people to be loved. We think we have failed unless we eliminate the burden. But the Bible doesn't say, "Remove one another's burdens." It says bear them.

Bearing is not something you can do for a few minutes and have it over with. Bearing suggests a commitment to long-term caring—and that not without pain.

At a recent crisis point in my life, I could easily have imagined I was living in the land of Uz, for Job's comforters promptly and eagerly volunteered their advice. They were well-meaning for the most part, but I think some were misguided. One man from the hierarchy of Moral Majority called from Washington asking to be told "all about it" so that he could "pray." Actually, as it turned out, he wrote me a letter telling me what I ought to do. I guess that was his way of burden-bearing.

Some responded with quick and half-informed criticism, prompting one of my colleagues to say, "Christians are the only people I know who shoot their wounded." I received a lot of how-to-fix-it books. A few people—thank God for the few—said, "I love you. I trust you. I am praying for you."

That experience taught me that burden-barers tend to focus on the problem, whereas the first concern of burden-bearers is the person. Thinking about this led me to examine carefully the context of the verse about burden-bearing.

This statement leaped out at me: "If a man should do something wrong, my brothers, you who are endowed with the

Spirit must set him right again very gently" (NEB). The King James translation, which says "in the spirit of meekness," had never hit me like "very gently." A meek bull in a china shop is still a bull. If there is no gentleness, I wondered, is there any Spirit-endowment? Also is not one who thinks and talks and acts with gentleness likely to have a quite different idea about what it means to "set right"? And about "baring"? And, for that matter about "wrong"?

Those who want to know "all about it" so they can "pray" should reconsider. Just a simple awareness of a need, no matter how many details are missing, is knowledge enough to pray lovingly and effectively. God, after all, does know. After an automobile accident, the paramedics don't need to know how it happened or who was at fault. Their concern is survival and healing. The attendant doesn't lean over the litter en route as the siren wails and red lights flash and say, "Tell me all about it." When the wounds are of the spirit and emotions, the retelling itself can tear open lesions that were perhaps just beginning to mend.

Christian counseling—which is another name for Christian caring—is not fast talking. It is slow listening. Since we are creatures of oral communication, we mistakenly think we have made no useful response unless we speak. Sometimes a pressure of the hand, an arm upon the shoulder, a silence shared—with no compulsion to come up with a solution—is the most eloquent encouragement.

I have a friend with a drinking problem. He used to call me long-distance day or night, but only when he was on a binge. He wouldn't take my advice to stop drinking. Finally, I quit taking his calls or returning them. I told him I'd done all I could. He stopped calling.

Nothing had "worked." It may have been because "doing" was not the point. I think now that caring could have been. Even as I write this, I have decided to call him.

Christians are embarrassed when others' failures contradict the image of piety and saintliness we have projected for ourselves and them. Our embarrassment produces a judgmental attitude. And that attitude, I'm convinced, drives burden-crushed ones back into lonely isolation and dishonest living.

I noticed something else in those Galatian verses. In the Living Bible it comes out as a caution signal to burden-barers: "Next time it might be one of you."

If so, you will then treasure, as I have, a few burden-bearers. And you, too, will take heart as they gather around you and begin singing brand new words to a grand old hymn:

> *Rise up, O church of God!*
> *This man for you doth wait,*
> *His strength unequal to his task,*
> *Rise up and make him great!*

Souls are for more than winning

What brought it to my attention was a letter from an elderly pastor in Poland. He told me about the small seminary where he is a teacher, and said, "My favorite subject to lecture is soul-caring."

I like that! I've heard a lot about soul-winning, but not very much about soul-caring. Apparently it's been hidden or missing for a long time, for even the psalmist lamented, "No man cared for my soul."

Caring.

Winning.

We can always care. We can't always win. It was said of the rich young ruler—Jesus' "unsuccessful" attempt at winning—that Jesus, "beholding him, loved him." Was that why the young man "went away sorrowful"? Was it his rejection of love that made the impact, or was it his rejection of eternal life (Mark 10:17–24)? It would be interesting to know where that young man finally wound up, what direction he ultimately chose for his life, whether searing memories of that encounter stayed with him down the years. Did he ever rearrange his priorities?

It is usually possible, I think, to know when one is loved,

when one's soul is being cared for rather than coveted. Soul-caring is always personal. There is a recognition across barriers, a glimpsing of oneself in the eyes into which one looks, a finding of likeness whatever outward difference. Soul-caring is the quiet but shattering discovery of mutuality. It is the transcending of narrow interest and status, a warm respect that suddenly links destinies. To care, one must become vulnerable, let someone else matter, surrender in some sense a measure of one's own sovereignty. That was the trouble with Jim Jones of Guyana. He was a soul-winner, but he was not a soul-carer. He captured souls; he did not free them.

With apologies to the translators of the King James Bible (some other translations do better), I am somewhat troubled by the way they handle Proverbs 11:30: "He that winneth souls is wise." It seems to me that "winning" is a self-directed concept. Caring is an other-directed concept. To win, you have to come in ahead of someone else. You are in competition. Do you remember this gospel song: "Will there be any stars in my crown?" I never thought of those "stars" as human beings in their own right. I saw them as decorations for me. I'd like to see the word "trophy" dropped from our evangelistic vocabulary, too. The word gives me the mental image of the heads of wild animals mounted in somebody's den and I want to be more than a display for some spiritual big-game hunter.

When the focus is on being a winner, the soul being won tends to become secondary, almost an afterthought.

"Winning" just may not be the best word. When we bring good news to someone in despair, we don't say we "win" the despairing one. We are more likely to say that we comfort or release or bless him or her, or whatever it is that happens to the person as a result of the message. If there is any "winner" in soul-winning, it is surely the one who hears and acts upon the good news, not the one who transmits it.

Soul-winning, as we commonly use the expression, often deals in numbers, fostering the impression that evangelicals are interested primarily in spiritual body counts or in getting a somewhat burdensome assignment over, with as little inconvenience as possible. We're not doing much thinking—or caring—about the earthly environment to which saved souls will have to return and in which they are expected to operate happily and victoriously with little further attention from us.

Soul-caring must go on not only after confrontation, but must precede it. Perhaps there are some evangelists who "win" with only superficial caring, but I hope they are in the minority. Perhaps there are congregations whose prime motivation for what they call evangelism is the increasingly desperate need to bolster a shaky budget, but this is no adequate solution to either financing or evangelizing. In the church, the bottom line has to be not intake but outgo—not snaring but caring.

There are still pouting Jonahs in the world who accuse God of softness when he accepts the repentance of a Nineveh these fire-breathers hope he will incinerate. But the nagging question remains: Does destruction or repentance offer the greater vindication of prophethood? Don't ask Jonah, for you will get the wrong answer. Thanks to the intervention of God, Jonah became a soul-winner, though an unintentional and even unwilling one. He knew little, it seems obvious, about soul-caring.

Some years ago, half the population–558 people–of a village in India embraced Islam. Asked why they preferred Islam to Christianity, the converts said that Christian concern for people ended with their conversion while the Islamic society looked after them even following their conversion.

I hope their perception is wrong or that it's different in other places. But I'm afraid it may not be.

If "winning" is all we are interested in, maybe we deserve the ones we are not getting. If we want to "win" without moving close to the lost one, without touching him, without sharing something of his life and hope and hurt, without venturing into his lostness, without trying to make him a friend before making him a convert (and not simply in order to make him a convert), we're going in the wrong direction, whatever the assistance of how-to seminars and computers and communication gimmicks.

Preaching, as you can see is eight-ninths (p)reaching, whether by an appointed minister in a pulpit or a lay Christian in daily life. Figuratively and literally, it could be said that if there is no reaching, there is no preaching. And it could also be said that if there is no caring, there is no reaching.

So the final question, then: Who cares?

The heresy of half-truth

"**D**o you swear to tell the truth, the whole truth . . . ?" are familiar words to anyone who has served on a jury. Perhaps the oath would be better worded, "Do you swear that whatever you tell will be true?" since the "whole" truth cannot easily be compressed into the testimony of one person.

The whole truth generally is not arrived at simply or without tension. My experience is that most often whole truth is made up of contradictory half-truths.

For example, Calvinists are absolutely certain that a sovereign God alone controls the destiny of man. Arminians are equally certain that man makes choices of his own volition. Election/free will. Is one right to the exclusion of the other? Or does the tension between them provide something greater than either by itself?

Look at some other half/whole truths: Law/grace, mercy/justice, forgiveness/judgment.

There are more than a few tension-producing biblical truths. How do you handle these two statements of Jesus: "Anyone who is not against you is for you" (Luke 9:50 LB) and "Anyone who is not for me is against me" (Luke 10:23 LB)? Or Isaiah 2:4: "They shall beat their swords into plowshares, and their spears into pruning hooks."? And Joel 3:10: "Beat your plowshares into swords, and your pruning hooks into spears"? There you have proof texts for both pacifists and militarists.

Can we understand Peter's confusion when after the Last Supper, Jesus said, "If you don't have a sword, better sell your clothes and buy one!" (Luke 22:36 LB), only to be told a few hours later, after he had slashed off a man's ear, "Put away your sword. Those using swords will get killed" (Matt. 26:52 LB)?

Church history has its examples, too. In the fourth century, the Docetics insisted that Jesus was not a real living man who shared our human situation and felt our hurts. Emphasizing his divinity, they said Jesus only seemed to have a human body and that he did not actually suffer and die on the cross. This was one manifestation of gnosticism, which was essentially a striving after system by men who felt impelled to bring all truth into absolute harmony—a temptation that to this day gets us into trouble.

Arianism, on the other hand, argued that the Son was a finite being, different from the Father in essence. In other words, he was not truly God. The Council of Nicaea was convened in 325 A.D. to sort out the half-truths and develop a statement reflecting the whole truth. Half of the picture alone constituted heresy. Only together—God/man, divine/human—did they constitute wholeness.

For me, Christian maturity is not trying to resolve the conflict between contradictory half-truths, but believing them both and holding them in appropriate tension. Heresy, it seems to me, results when you discard one facet of truth in favor of another facet of the same truth.

In the West, we have gotten our philosophy from the mentally tidy Greeks who found it hard to live with contradictory truth. They said, "If A is A, then A is not non-A." Thus A and B were mutually exclusive and irreconcilable. Agreeing with the Greeks, we find it hard to tolerate tension in truth. We have this compulsion to resolve everything into neat black-or-white categories, the sooner the better.

The rest of the world, including the world where Jesus lived, can more easily accept the gray ambiguity of real life. The Chinese, for example, don't have our trouble. When two people disagree in principle, they say, "A is right and B is not wrong." But because our faith is a propositional faith, we decided to build it on the nonambiguity of Hellenistic thought, forgetting that before faith is a proposition, it is a relationship.

In the physical world, competing tensions hold everything in place and you need only to look into the night sky to see how it works. Eliminate the pull of one planet and all the planets would move into new relationships. It is earth's reaction to these pulls, and its own contribution, that literally makes the world go around.

What if we learned to use creatively the tensions of real life in our relationships instead of trying to eliminate them? What if, in church and family, instead of some one person, some one viewpoint, *having* to be right, we could gratefully admit that it may take several viewpoints to encompass "right"?

Evangelicals really have trouble with that approach. When you "have the truth," it is so easy to judge. The Pharisees, who thought they had an exclusive franchise on truth, could lay it on both Jesus and John. Jesus describes them this way: "For John the Baptist doesn't even drink wine and often goes without food, and you say, 'He's crazy.' And I, the Messiah, feast and drink, and you complain that I am a glutton and a drinking man and hang around with the worst sort of sinners" (Matt. 11:18–19 LB).

Could Jesus be saying, "John is right and I am not wrong"? He sarcastically concludes: "But brilliant men like you can justify your every inconsistency!" Inconsistency was all right, but paradox was not acceptable.

Is there then no such thing as an eternal verity? Of course

there is, but it resides in a Person, not in a proposition. Jesus is *the* Truth. My beliefs may be true or they may be only my partial and biased interpretation of truth, but whichever, they are relative to the Absolute and I do well to treat them with more humility and less arrogance.

Otherwise, I have joined the joyless circle of those who, since time began, thought their own little piece of truth was all the truth there was.

Heresy, they called it, when it happened long ago.

Perhaps it is still the right word.